I0469565

# The Ultimate Sales System For

# Professionals

The only system you'll ever need to become wildly successful at selling without looking like a money-hungry, greedy, conniving, bait-and-switch, pushy, snake-oil salesman

Author and Business Coach

## David L. Sims

ISBN: 1481876473
ISBN-13: 978-1481876476

# CONTENTS

# INTRODUCTION AND OVERVIEW

One of the most common beliefs about selling is that "Selling is something you do to people and not something that is beneficial for them." If you believe this concept and it's deeply ingrained within your subconscious, then you'll find it extremely difficult to sell your products or services to anyone.

You may not think you are in sales. But think about this, ***"Every personal encounter you have is actually a sales encounter. Every encounter, every communication, every interaction is a sales presentation. In every encounter, someone sells and someone buys."*** You succeed in life according to your ability to sell your ideas. You sell your children on a good education. You sell your family on living the good life. If you are a man and you ask a woman out for a date, that's a sales presentation. If you make an excellent sales presentation she might buy. If you don't then she'll sell you... and say "NO!"

If you have children and you want them to clean their room. You make a sales presentation. They either buy or sell. **"In every encounter a sales presentation is made. Either you buy or you sell. It's that simple."** The more you study psychology, communication and the selling process, the more successful you'll be with achieving your life goals.

## Selling can really be boiled down to a simple concept.

**"If people don't feel better about themselves after you've left their presence then they did before you arrived, you won't sell them."**

The definition of selling is this, "**Selling is an exchange of ideas**." It goes as follows, "You have an idea about how your product or service will help make your client or prospect enjoy a better life.  Now here's the question, *"will they be willing to listen to your idea?"*  And more importantly, will they like your idea enough to pay you to implement it?"

Before you get started into the nuts and bolts of selling, there are some truths about selling for you to understand.  I call these "axioms" because they are universal truths.  I've made a list for your review. After you review this list you may want to give up the study of selling and become a shelf stocker at one of the major retailers.  If you want a prosperous career, read on.

Selling is conceptual.  Your success is really determined more about **how you feel about yourself** then the technical knowledge you possess. Selling is conceptual and Your success in selling usually depends upon how much PSYCHOLOGICAL BAGGAGE you're carrying around between your ears.

The more baggage you're carrying around the harder it will be for you to be successful developing a career in sales.  You can over come that "baggage" by reprogramming your subconscious mind.

# CHAPTER 1
# THE TEN TRUTHS ABOUT SELLING YOU SHOULD KNOW

**Sales Truth #1:** *"You Must Have A Quality Product Or Service To Present To Your Prospect Or Client."*

If your product or service is less than par then it will be a struggle for you to build a long term client base. You may be a good enough salesperson to make a few sales but when the word gets around that you don't deliver quality service or a good product, it won't be long before no one will buy. You must deliver the goods. The first part of the equation is to have a quality product or service. If you provide a bad product or bad service it won't take long for the word to get around. An unhappy customer will tell 10-12 people about the "bad experience" they had with you. On the other hand if you have a good product or service your clients will only tell 4-5 people about their happiness with you.

**Sales Truth #2:** *"People Must Like You Before They'll Do Business With You."*

As a general rule, "if people don't like you they won't do business with you." I know there may be a time when you "have to" do business with people you don't like, but not very often. Maybe in a "closed bid" situation where it is a true closed bid (most of them aren't), you may end up doing business with someone you don't like. But in life we all make choices. You may choose to take money from someone and make that person a client even if you don't like them.

You may justify this by saying "you need the money really badly." The real truth of the matter is you probably don't have a good enough marketing system to feed you enough clients so you can pick and choose the ones you want to work with. I know this has happened to me and I took on clients because I "thought" I needed the money so bad I couldn't pass them up. The real truth of the matter is they actually cost me money because I developed such a negative attitude from putting up with them I drove other clients away.

One of the beginning parts of the sales process is to bond with people. You need to build rapport with them in order to get them to like you. As Dale Carnegie stated many, many years ago, *"people don't care how much you know until they know how much you care."*

You must learn how to sell to different personality styles. Each personality style communicates differently and buys differently. You need to give each prospect whatever personality they want to see in order to sell them. There are about four different personalities you'll be selling to. I cover this more later in the book when I get to the part about "Building Rapport."

## Sales Truth #3: *"People Must Trust You Before They'll Do Business With You."*

Trust is crucial in any selling situation. You can't have too much credibility or trust. In order to convince someone to become your client you must first establish an environment of trust. That can be done many ways. If you're an expert in your field that help's establish credibility. If you have articles published that will help create credibility.

Writing a book, will go a long way towards creating credibility and trust. You may be speaking to a group on your particular subject and someone from the audience seeks you out. They do so because you have credibility because you're able to speak in front of a group of people. Most people are scared stiff of speaking in front of any group, (It's often listed as the number one fear in America) even if they're your friends or colleagues.

**"The most effective way to create trust is to be referred to the prospect by someone who has influence with the prospect."**

One of the best methods of creating trust is to use testimonials. **One of the most <u>Underused methods</u> of establishing trust and credibility is acquiring testimonials from an enthusiastic client.** Testimonials are essential for any marketing material you use. Testimonials should be included in your brochures, web sites, or any ads you place, or direct marketing you do. When you're meeting in person with a prospect you should show them as many testimonials as you have.

I have a bound book over an inch in thickness containing many, many testimonials. I give this book, along with other marketing materials, to a new *prospect* before I ever meet with them. I highlight the specific benefits the clients received and listed in the testimonials. This will be a great tool in helping to overcome any objections any prospect might have.

This is a fantastic way to overcome objections before your prospect can bring them up. There are probably only 3 or 4 objections anyone would have for not doing business with you. A great set of testimonials will go a long way to helping overcome these objections.

This is so important I'm going to mention it again. A great way to create instant trust with your prospect is to *"Get referred to the prospect by someone who has influence with them. Get the person referring you to introduce you to the prospect and then set the appointment for you. That creates instant trust." (When you learn to do this you'll sell over 70% to 80% of the people you call on.)*

This is the way I get referred to several business people. I have the people referring me to contact the decision maker on my behalf and introduce me before I ever meet with them. When you use this approach it's almost 100% guaranteed you'll get an appointment, you'll have a great meeting, and you'll close over 80% of your sales interviews.

## Sales Truth #4: *"There Is No Such Thing As A Bad Prospect, Only Bad Sales Techniques."*

One thing you may have found in the past is the prospect actually knows more about the selling system than you do. I hope you are able to correct that with the help of this book. However, that's not uncommon. For what ever reason, the prospect knows more about the selling process than sales people do. The real truth about selling is that selling is nothing more than, **"a Broadway play put on by a psychiatrist."** You must know psychology to know how to interact with the prospect. There are a lot of dynamics to the selling process and the one major key needed is to know how to communicate effectively with different people.

You definitely need to have a wide range of communication skills. I'll introduce you to those in the discovery section. But if you don't possess a wide range of communication skills, (listening skills, being empathetic, ability to ask good questions, and having high self-esteem and a high self-image) you will have a tough time with the prospect because they'll run the show and you'll feel helpless.

For example: Let's say you're talking to a prospect and one of the first questions they ask you is, "what do you charge?" Maybe you're not ready to talk about money yet because of several different reasons. If you're unskilled in the art of selling you may blurt out what you charge for your product or service. The prospect then replies, *"That's way to much money. Number one we don't have it in the budget and number two I wouldn't spend that much money for your product or service because I can get it cheaper elsewhere."*

If that happens, you're sunk. You take your pretty four-color brochures and other material and leave. Before you leave you leave a brochure and business card and say something like, "I'll leave some material for you and if you change your mind, give me a call." But they rarely ever do.

I'm going to give you a lot of information in this book. If you want to be sure this never happens to you, you must practice, drill and rehearse to ensure it doesn't happen. Here's a great way to handle the question, "How much do you charge?" Especially if you're not to the point where you want to talk about money yet. You simply say, *"Mister prospect you're on page seven and I'm only on page three. Do you mind if I catch up with you before we begin talking about money? In order for me to do that I need to ask you a few questions. Is that O.K?"* Then you begin asking probing questions.

(You'll learn more techniques later about developing skills of asking questions.)

## Sales Truth #5: *"Price Is Never An Objection When Making A Sale. If People Are In Enough Pain They Will Pay Anything To Get Rid Of It!"*

One of the hardest concepts I had to learn in selling is this, "people don't buy intellectually." I thought if I gave a brilliant presentation the prospects would be so blown away by it that the presentation would be all I needed to make a sale. Boy was I wrong. I later found out that "people buy emotionally and then justify it intellectually or logically.

The old concept of a Class A prospect is this:

*Someone who has a need for your product or service.

9

*Someone who has money to buy what you offer.

*Someone that can make a buying decision.

I found later in my selling career that if you could uncover a prospects "**PAIN**" they would be willing to pay anything to get rid of it. (That is if they have any money. I tried to sell to some people who didn't have money and no matter how much pain I uncovered, they couldn't and wouldn't buy.)

I even tried to sell by being the lowest bidder. Do you want to know what happened? If I did make the sale two things occurred. First, my margins were so narrow I didn't make much money. Second, as soon as someone came by with a lower price than mine, my client left and went with them.

I eventually found out that the most effective way to sell was to **uncover the pain** the prospect had filed away. (You do that by being good at asking compelling questions.) Then the sale was much easier to make and money became less of an issue.

Here's why it was less of an issue. I first talked about what was important to them. I did that by asking several questions to uncover the pain. Most sales people want to begin the selling process by <u>"presenting and trying to sell before they ever find out if there is a pain they can fix."</u> That's a tough way to make money selling because now you're selling by the law of averages. You've probably had an owner or sales manager tell you, "selling is a numbers game.

If you call on 100 people and sell one the only thing you have to do is to call on 1000 people to sell 10." Yes it's a numbers game but most people have to call on such a large number of prospects to sell enough to make money they usually go broke and quit before they develop their profession.

If you can't uncover any pain then you are left to sell to an intellectual buyer. Now you begin selling by being the lowest bidder. Remember, people buy emotionally and justify it logically. The most effective way is to become an expert at asking good, compelling questions, become skilled at listening, and become an expert at psychology. That's when you'll begin to earn a great income.

## Sales Truth #6: *"Sell First, Educate Later."*

Have you ever educated a prospect for free? I believe everyone in sales has been an unpaid consultant at one time or another. What that means is this, they ask you questions about how to solve their problem. Your thinking is this, "if I help them by giving them free information they'll probably give me their business." **Nothing could be farther from the truth.** They'll take your information and run to your competitor to beat them down to a lower price than what you're charging. Then they'll come back to you and beat you down even farther.

Here's what happens. They ask you how you would solve their problem and how much you would charge to do that. They then take that information to your competitor and ask for a quote from the information you just gave them. Your competitor gives them a quote. The prospect then tells your competitor they must talk to you before making a decision. The prospect now has a price from your competitor lower that what you charge. They come back to you with the lower price and tell you, "If you want the business you must come in below your competitor."

You lose and your competitor loses. The one coming out on top is the prospect. You must find out if they will give you their business if you propose a solution to solve their problem.

You must find out three items before you ever give them your fee.

**\*First, you must find out if they have any PAIN.**

**\*Second, you must find out if they have a BUDGET set up to pay for your product or service.**

**\*Third, you must find out the DECISION MAKING PROCESS they use to reach a final decision.**

These are the three "MUSTS" that you have to do before you ever present any solutions or investments numbers to them. You'll learn more about this when you get to the **"Discovery Process"** later in the book. But here's an essential key to selling. If you present your solution to their problem and the price you're going to charge before you find out these three key components, **"You'll fail 80%-90% of the time!"**

But please, don't fall into the trap of being an unpaid consultant. You've worked long and hard to acquire your knowledge and skills. Don't give it away!

# Sales Truth #7: *"Telling Ain't Selling, Asking Questions Is."*

Often you'll hear someone say, "She could sell ice to an Eskimo." They say that because the person they're talking about talks a lot and people often equate "talking with selling." In fact the opposite is true. You are more effective at selling if you talk less than your prospect. As a rule of thumb, if you're in the selling interview, you should talk 20% to 30% of the time. The prospect should talk 70% to 80% of the time.

Think about this. You already know what you know. You want to know what the prospect knows. You want to know what pains they have. You want to know what's important to them. You want to know their money situation. You want to know their decision making process. You can't find that information out if you are talking non-stop.

In order to set the stage where your prospect is talking most of the time, you have to become excellent at asking questions. You then must also be excellent at listening. You want to listen for what they say and sometimes you want to listen for what they don't say. (Maybe there's a question they should be asking you but they haven't.)

You should practice asking questions all the time. Most of the questions you ask will begin with, "Who, what, where, when, how, and why." You should always be empathetic for your prospect. You must also be nurturing. When you meet someone new and are interviewing them for the first time, you always want to begin with questions that are easy to answer and non-threatening. You must build trust and rapport before you move on to more probing questions.

If the prospect doesn't like you or trust you, they will either evade your questions or they will lie to you. One of the first keys to become effective at asking questions is to establish an environment of trust with your prospect. Instant trust is created if you're referred to the prospect by someone having influence with them.

If you aren't referred to them then it will take time to build trust. The trust environment is established in several ways. One way is by your body language. You must appear non-threatening by the way you sit or stand. Second, You never want to ask a question of the prospect they don't know the answer to. Third, you don't want to use too much technical language the prospect doesn't understand. If you do you'll make them feel very uncomfortable.

**You must begin your interview with short easy to answer questions.** This will help build trust with the prospect because you are beginning to make they feel comfortable. Also, you're giving them a chance to talk about themselves which they don't often get an opportunity to do.

It may take more than one meeting to build trust with the prospect. But until you build that environment of trust the prospect won't answer your questions truthfully.

## Sales Truth #8: *"You Are Now Earning Exactly What You Think You're Worth. Not A Penny More, Not A Penny Less!"*

When you were very young, as young as one year of age, your **belief systems** were being formed. And that system has continually been added to every day since then. **Your belief system is the system you live with every day.** Your belief system is like a "thermostat" that governs your success. If your belief system tells you that you will be successful, then you will be successful. If your belief system tells you that you can't be successful or that you don't deserve success or that the "deck" is always stacked against your succeeding, then you won't succeed.

Your subconscious will sabotage your success. It will automatically adjust your success to your perception of what you deserve. If you've ever played poker or watched some of the tournaments on TV you know that the odds of drawing to an inside straight and begin successful are very slim. So it is in life if your "success-regulating thermostat" is telling you that you don't deserve to succeed, you may enjoy a little success but your belief "thermostat" will adjust and you will sabotage your own success.

You may experience a little success for awhile but your "self-esteem" will adjust your success back to your "comfort zone." You have to change the set of your "success thermostat" before you can change your success.

Are you familiar with how a "thermostat" works? You have a thermostat in your home that regulates the temperature or "Comfort Zone" in your house. In the winter time the thermostat controls the heating unit.

Suppose you want your "Comfort Zone" to be 70 degrees Fahrenheit. That's where you set your thermostat. When the temperature in your room drops below 70 degrees the thermostat sends a message to the brain in the heating unit and tells it, *"We're getting uncomfortable so you need to turn on the heat."* The unit then turns the heat on and begins to warm the house.

When the house heats up to 70 degrees, and gets back in the comfort zone, the thermostat then sends a message to the heating unit (brain) and tells it to turn off until further notice. The same happens when you have an air conditioning unit. In the summertime you turn your cooling unit on and set your thermostat to the desired temperature. Lets say that you again set your temperature to 70 degrees. The temperature in the room begins to heat up and now the thermostat tells the air conditioning unit to turn on and begin cooling the room.

When the temperature cools down to 70 degrees the thermostat then tells the unit to turn off until further notice. This is the way your self-esteem works to regulate your success. You have a "comfort zone" for your success. When you reach that "comfort zone," your subconscious mind tells you that it's time to relax and take it easy. Or it may even convince you that you're sick and need to take it easy a few days.

You have a built in mechanism that regulates your success. It's called your **self-esteem.** Your self-esteem is made up of all the past programming you've received to this point in your life. You've received information from your family, friends, church, schools, the TV you've watched, the things you've listened to and the information you've read. However, and this is very important to understand, the people you associate with have a tremendous influence on how you think and feel about yourself. The main five people you associate with should be in a position of success you want to achieve. These all contribute to your self-esteem. The challenge you face with the development of your self-esteem is, "you had very little input or control about how you were programmed when you were younger."

## "You Can Change Your Self-Esteem And Self-Image If You Choose To Do So!"

You may try to become more successful by overriding your "self-esteem" with will power. However, you can't override your self-esteem.

**You have to reprogram it.** There are only three ways you can get out of your comfort zone.

*First, **you must be inspired** to get out of your comfort zone. You do this with a good, solid, written goals plan. Unfortunately, only about 5% of Americans have a written goals plan. You must have a good, goals plan that you focus on regularly to get you out of your comfort zone. It is a basic fundamental of success. You might be inspired by a speech, a song, a movie, or someone's story.

*Second, **you may become desperate.** If you are desperate you may try things you wouldn't do otherwise because you were too concerned what others would think. Or your being desperate might override your comfort zone because you're emotionally sick and tired of the way your life is and you're going to take action to change it. (Your comfort zone is your biggest detriment to your success. You'll subconsciously do almost anything to stay in your comfort zone.)

*Third, you may have a religious conversion. When you do you'll have a completely different philosophy about life and your activities and your habits. You may rely on a higher power than yourself to change to the behavior you need to become successful but can you really afford to wait for that to happen?

Almost every training program you'll ever attend will focus on "technical training." If you take a sales training course the material will focus on the technical aspect of selling. What I mean by that is they'll focus on:

*The technical skills to overcome objections.

*The technical skills to ask questions.

*The technical skills to give presentations to present your product or service.

*The technical skills needed to put together a dynamic proposal.

Those all may be helpful but the most important part of training you need is to reprogram your self-esteem and self-image. (A great source for doing this is a book by Maxwell Maltz titled, "Psychocybernetics.")

If you have low self-esteem or a low self-image then you won't be able to handle much rejection and in sales you'll get a lot of rejection. If you get a couple of prospects saying "NO" at the beginning of the day you'll have a tendency to avoid any more calls the rest of the day if you have a low self-esteem or low self-image.

If you have high self-esteem and high self-image and someone tells you "NO" at the beginning of the day your attitude is, That "NO" is just one step closer to a sale. I can't wait until I get the next "NO" because I know I'm getting closer and closer to a sale."

## Sales Truth #9: *"You Can't Get Upset At A Prospect For Doing Something You Didn't Tell Them They Couldn't Do!"*

Selling is like a going to the dentist. You've probably gone to a dentist at one time or another. In the old days of dentistry it was a scary event because you wouldn't know what was going to happen. The dentist would set you in a chair and take a sharp looking probe and begin digging in your teeth. If they were going to do anything that needed much work they would inject you with a needle that looked like something that grandma used to crochet with. It was scary because of all the unknowns that the dentist was going to do.

Is this day and age when you go to a dentist it's a different experience. The dentist leads you through the entire process and tells you exactly what's going to happen before every step of the way. The dentist will let you know exactly what's going to happen each step of the process. When they do that it makes it an easier experience because you know exactly what to expect.

Selling is like dancing. Someone needs to lead and someone needs to follow. If you are the one leading in the sales process you need to tell the prospect what they can expect each step of the way.

For example the first time you meet with your prospect you can tell them what to expect from your first meeting. You want to find out about the prospect and you want the prospect to find out about you. If the prospect has a problem you feel you can solve and they want to visit with you about it then tell them you'll talk about their situation.

Each step of the way you tell them what will happen in advance. If they ask you to put together a proposal, you then clarify what they want to see in the proposal. When they tell you what they want then ask what will happen when you put it together. Get them to agree to say "YES" or "NO". But then you also get them to agree to not tell you they want to think it over about making a decision.

In every sales interview you should get one of four things to happen. A "YES," a "NO," a LESSON, or a REFERRAL. If you settle for "I want to think it over." Or, "I need to visit with my wife or husband." Or some other form of a stall, they will drive you crazy and you'll go broke. You may not make the sale on the first call. If you're going back for a second call you can ask for a commitment.

Here's the commitment you ask for. "Mr./Ms. Prospect I'll come back on the agreed date and bring you the proposal. Can I ask you a question? When I come back will you agree to make a "Yes" or "No" decision? And a "No" is O.K. But what I would like to request you not to do is to say, "I want to think it over." "Will you agree to that?"

When you can get prospects to agree to this decision to say either "Yes" or "No" instead of "I want to think it over." You sales will skyrocket.

## Sales truth #10: *"Your Attitude Going Into A Sales Interview Will Usually Determine The Outcome Of The Sales Interview."*

Your attitude is extremely important for your sales success. To be successful you need to be self-confident. You also need to have the attitude and the mantra; *"I'm financially independent and I don't need this* _**business.**_ If you're hurting for a sale and you desperately need the sale for the money, your prospect can sense that subconsciously and they'll back away and many won't buy.

You have three key components that will make up a successful attitude.

*First, you must have a great attitude about yourself. You must believe in yourself and have a good amount of self confidence. To be successful at selling you need to work on your attitude continually. 80% to 90% of all the information your exposed to daily is <u>negative</u>. It's extremely difficult to become successful in selling with a negative attitude.

If you want to succeed in selling you must continually work on maintaining a positive, optimistic attitude about yourself.

*Second, you must have a good attitude about your company, your product, and the people you work with or work for.

*Third, you must have a good attitude about your marketplace. If you don't like your marketplace, if you don't feel it's a viable place to sell, it will make it tougher to succeed.

When you combine these three elements you have the recipe for becoming successful in sales. The three attitudes are important. The most important is the ,"Attitude about yourself." It will comprise about 80% of the attitude triangle. The attitude about your product will make up about 10% of the triangle. The attitude about your marketplace will make up the other 10% of the triangle.

You must continually work on your attitude daily. Read inspirational material daily. Read your affirmations daily. Read your goals on a regular basis. Listen to uplifting music. Don't watch or read too much news. That usually is 100% negative.

A great way to work on maintaining your positive, optimistic attitude is to create a recording of many of your achievements you've experienced through the years. Listen to this on a regular basis for a shot of optimism.

# CHAPTER 2
# WHAT IS THE NUMBER ONE KEY TO YOUR SELLING SUCCESS?

In my study and search to become excellent and master the selling skills needed to earn an excellent income, I've spent in excess of one hundred thousand dollars on books, audio materials, video materials, workshops, and coaching. I was continually searching for the "Magic Pill" for success. How do you think I felt when I found out, "**There's no magic pill for success**?" What really hurt was the person giving me that information was the man I'd recently paid over $50,000.00 to for that answer and for a business opportunity.

The only key you need to know for your success is this, "**The beginning point of your success is very simply. You Must Take Personal Responsibility For Your Success.**" Your destiny and control is in your hands and no other. Even in times of economic hardships and recession there are skilled salespeople earning an excellent income.

You can't blame your neighbors, the government, inflation, your relatives, or taxes. You must understand the beginning point is this; **You Must Take Personal Responsibility For Your Success And For Your Failure.** It's wrapped up in your personal philosophy.

All the daily actions you generate are a result of the habits you've formed over the years plus your belief systems. My belief is that all behavior is learned behavior. If you want a new action, a new result, a new behavior, or a new habit you have the power of choice. You can choose to take action or choose not to take action. You can literally change the results you achieve by changing the way you think.

When you attend a seminar you may have fun, get excited, or get a new idea. Studies show that after 2 weeks you remember less than 10% of the information you were exposed to. Studies also show that if you don't take action within 48 hours there's a 70% chance you won't take any action. If you don't take action within 72 hours the chances you won't take action are over 90%.

How do you make a change in behavior? You must use spaced repetition and reinforcement. When you attempt an action, you have either a degree of success or failure. You practice, study, rehearse, make adjustments and try again. You do this over and over. This is the way to change a behavior, to form a new habit.

### Every Achievement In Life Begins With An Idea.

You must begin with a **VISION**. Every achievement, every accomplishment, every invention ever created began with an idea, or in other words, A VISION. To understand how the **Success Pathway** works you must begin at the end of the pathway and work backwards. It's similar to building a house. You must first imagine the end product. Imagine the end product being a completed house. You then move backwards from the finished product to the to the very beginning, the **IDEA, THE DREAM, OR THE VISION.** Or as Stephen Covey say**s, "You must begin with the end in mind."**

The same is true for success. You must begin where you are right now and work backwards to find out how you came to this place in the beginning. When you complete that process you will then know what you need to do to change your life.

This is how you begin. The beginning step is to take a current assessment of where you are now. In other word you must assess **"Your Current Degree Of Success In Life."**

1. **Your Degree Of Success In Life**. At this very moment you are enjoying a degree of success in life. It may be the success you wanted or it may not. The concept to understand here is that you have a certain degree of success. The richest person in the world has a degree of success. The bum laying passed out on Commercial Street has a certain degree of success.

     You have a degree of success that you've achieved in your life. That is where you are this very moment. The really important thing to understand is that you are recognizing where you are and the first step to change is to understand that there is a better way or a different way.

(So the first Step in the process is to recognize "Your Current Degree of Success".)

2. **Results**....Step two is to understand that "your current degree of success" is generated by the results you produce every day. Every day you produce certain results. You may produce goal-achieving results or you may produce results that end in no accomplishment at all. Or you may even produce results that are detrimental to your mental or physical health. But every day of your life you produce some result. (Producing no results is actually a result).

3. **Actions**....What produces your results? Your results come from the different **actions** you take every day. If you read a book a week about success or about how someone became

successful, and then implement some of the actions that will produce results. If you don't do any of this and you only read one book a year, then that action will also produce a result. It may not be the result you are looking for but it will be a result. (It's difficult to read only one book a year and keep up). Your results in life depend on the **actions** you take daily. If you really, really want to be successful you must take "massive action." That could mean reading a book a day.

(I want to recommend a great book to you. "Action, Nothing Happens Until Something Moves". By Robert Ringer. You'll find out that the people who are most successful are the ones who take a lot of different **actions** to move them in the direction of their focus).

4.  **Behavior**…..<u>What is it that determines the actions you take each and every day</u>? It's your **behavior.** Behavior comes from the word, **"behave."** Webster's definition for **"behave"** is, "To act in a certain way." Every day you will "act in a certain way." Your behavior will produce certain actions, which produce your results. Your behavior can be affected by several different influences.

It could be a person in your life; Someone you admire or someone you look up to. A movie could affect your behavior. A movie. A book. You most probably developed your behavior by the programming you received as you grew up. It probably started as early as the first year of your life. The unfortunate thing about all our programming when we're young is that no one consulted us when they did our programming.

5. **Habits**....What is it that determines your behavior? Your **Habits**. Again, Webster's definition of "habit" is, "a tendency to perform a certain action or behave in a certain way.

    Your habits were formed years ago. Your habits cause you to perform subconsciously. For you to change one of your habits, you must do it consciously. Maybe you've heard that if you perform a certain action 21 days in a row then it'll become a habit. I don't agree with that. You may do something 21 days in a row that you don't like to do. But that action is necessary for you to achieve certain goals. Studies show that you need to repeat an action for at least 30 days for it to have an impact on you.

    If you no longer want to achieve "that goal," you'll stop performing that certain action. You must be motivated to continue with the action because usually the actions you must take to achieve your goals are hard to do plus they're undesirable to do. The reason they're hard for you to do is that they're uncomfortable for you. If they weren't uncomfortable for you, wouldn't you already be doing them???

6. **Attitude**.....Your **attitude** determines your habits. A habit is nothing more than a pattern of thought. A great slogan for an affirmation to keep with you at all times is, *"It's your attitude not your aptitude that determines your altitude".* Your attitude has been constructed over the years. The people you associate with, the books you read, the TV you watch, etc. All of the past programming you've experienced goes into making up your attitude.

One of the best sayings I've ever encountered was create years ago by Zig Ziglar. He said, *"You are where you are and what you are by what's gone into your mind."* He then went on to say, *"You can change where you are and what you are by changing what goes into your mind."*

7. **The Way You Think Controls All Of Your Success!** The way you think, your belief systems, your perception of life, your ideas and thoughts all contribute to your success. Your self-esteem and belief in yourself control your success and relationships in life. If you feel you deserve success and need success, (whatever success means to you), then you'll achieve it.

You can't help but achieve it. Your mind won't let you do anything else but that. If you don't believe you deserve success then your mind will do everything it can to defeat you. It will sabotage your relationships, it'll control your health, it'll control your activity, and it'll control your thinking.

The interesting thing about humans is that we guard our living rooms with gusto to keep people from dumping garbage in them. However, we open our minds daily and invite friends, relatives, and strangers. We invite them to massively dump tons of garbage in our minds daily to keep us from succeeding to the level our creator intended us too.

(An interesting note: Humans are the only mammals who don't live up to the full potential our creator instilled in us.)

EXERCISE:

**Here's a great exercise for you.**

Take a piece of notebook paper and draw a line down the middle of the paper. Label that line "NOW" and put today's date on it. Now draw a five-inch line perpendicular to the left of the line you drew down the center of the paper. Label the left end of the five-inch line, "five years ago." Think about the success and all the accomplishments you've achieved in the past five years.

Now draw a five-inch line to the right of the centerline and label it "five years into the future."

Here's the key: <u>"Your Next Five Years Will Look Exactly Like Your Last Five Years"</u> except for two things: **The Books You Read And The People You Meet.**

Your **attitude** is key to your success. I'm not referring to a positive, Pollyanna attitude. I'm referring to your attitude about yourself, your life, your work, your company, your marketplace, etc. Your **attitude** must be positive, optimistic, and full of self-confidence that you can accomplish anything you set your mind to. One of the biggest stumbling blocks to becoming successful is, **"lack of self-confidence."**

In reality you can change your Degree Of Success by changing any of the elements in this pathway. If you want to change your degree of success, you can do so by changing your "Behavior." You can change it by changing your "Habits." You can definitely change your Degree Of Success by changing "What Goes Into your Mind."

**<u>So Let's Summarize.</u>**

*What goes into your mind determines your attitude.

*Your attitude determines your habits.

*Your habits determine your behavior (behaviors are habits or patterns of thought);

*Your behavior determines your actions.

*The actions you take determine your results.

*Your results determine your degree of success in life.

Do you see the pathway for your success?

Now the last question is this. How do you change your attitude? (Your attitude is the way you think). Your attitude is determined by how you think. And how you think is determined by what goes into your mind.

Do you remember Zig Ziglar's quote? *"You are where you are and what you are because of what goes into our mind." You can change where you are and what you are by changing what goes into your mind."*

Here's the amazing thing about this process, you can create a shortcut! You can change your success by changing what you feed into your mind. Your mind is like a garden. If you plant a seed of corn in good fertile soil and water it you'll get corn in return. However, you won't get just one grain of corn, you'll get many multiples of that grain of corn you planted. If you plant a poison plant, like nightshade in your garden, you'll get nightshade in return. However, you won't get just one plant you'll get many.

If you plant negative thoughts, and remember, it is easier to think negatively than it is to think positively, you'll get negative in return. But it'll multiply. 80% to 90% of everything you're exposed to daily is negative. The majority of news, conversations with your friends, colleagues, relatives, or neighbors is negative. It is a tremendous challenge to constantly feed your mind with positive information.

If you plant "negative" in your mind, you'll get negative in return. But it'll multiply just like a garden. If you plant positive in your mind it'll return positive but many times over. A giant part of success is to think in positive, optimistic terms, self-confident, can do terms

# CHAPTER 3
# HOW GOAL SETTING AFFECTS YOUR SALES CAREER AND SUCCESS.

*"If you're not making the progress you'd like to make and think you're capable of making it's simply because your goals are not clearly defined."* Paul J. Meyer

## Question:  What critical factor will determine your level of success?

## Answer:  You Must Become An Expert At Setting And Accomplishing Goals!

> ## "The Number One Activity Responsible For Your Achievement Is GOAL SETTING."

Unfortunately goal setting isn't taught in our schools at any level, not grade school, high school, or college.  In the United States less than 15% of people are active goal setters.  Less than 5% have a written goals program.  Long-term studies show if you commit your goals in writing you have a 95% greater chance of accomplishing them than if you don't convert your goals to written form.

Several years ago a study was conducted at Harvard.  One of the staff was interested in the economic groups in the U.S.  After extensive study he found:

*That 3% of the people in this country were wealthy.

*10% Lived comfortable

*60% Just get by.

*27% Needed support to survive.

He was startled by these results. Here we live in the richest country in the world and only 13% really and truly enjoyed financial success. He was puzzled and studied farther. What he found was this, it's a behavior issue tied to Goal Setting. He found that the top "13%" were goal-setters. And the other 87% were not "goal-setters."

Upon farther study he divided the top 13% into two groups. The top 3%, or the wealthy group, had a **Written Specific Goals Plan.** The other 10% had goals but no written plan or a tracking system for their goals. They were goal driven and had goals in mind but not specific plan.

The 60% group spent more time planning their summer vacation than they did planning their life or success. This group would get brochures about vacation sites, travel plans, shows to see once they got there, etc. But when it came to setting goals at the beginning of the year for different accomplishments, they were pretty much non existence.

Now you may be asking why I'm including a session on Goal-Setting in a sales book. Here's the answer. There is no profession you'll ever be involved in that will have as much rejection as the sales profession. If you're really successful you may not succeed over 30% of the time. In other words if you were a baseball player and could get 3 hits for every 10 at bats, you'd be a multimillionaire.

If you can sell 3 out of 10 presentations you'll also do very well. So tell me what other profession do you know of where the employees or professionals get rejected 70% of the time? The goals plan is necessary to keep you getting up everyday to go out and play the sales game. If you don't have strong goals that you'll achieve when you're successful at selling it will be tough for you to continue and not quit. I've seen more people fail at selling then I've seen succeed.

## What Are The Critical Components

## For A Successful Goals Program?

To begin with the first three components needed are:

<u>First:</u> You must have a **Specific goal.**

<u>Second:</u> You must have a **Measurement System** to keep track of your progress. **(If you can't measure it, you can't manage it.)**

<u>Third:</u> You must have a **Time frame** for the achievement of your goal.

(Deadlines are critical to your success. They create urgency.)

*First you must define a **Specific Goal**– When you have a specific target, not a vague, general description, you're using the "rifle approach" to achieve your goals. The major benefit from this approach is you will achieve your goal much faster. The reason for this is you are aiming at a specific target and it's easier to stay on track. If you use the "shotgun approach" you may accomplish your goal but it'll be much more difficult and more time consuming. The "shotgun approach" is a vague, general approach.

## Examples:

General – My goal is to be rich; or my goal is to be wealthy.

Specific – My goal is to have 1 million dollars in the bank with an annual income of $100,00.00 by the time I'm 50 years old.

---------------------------------------------------------------

General – My goal is to see more prospects.

Specific – My goal is to call on one additional prospect a day for the next 90 days.

---------------------------------------------------------------

General – I want to be healthier.

Specific – My goal is to be ten pounds thinner, and run a mile in 8 minutes by the end of 90 days.

---------------------------------------------------------------

*Measurement System - The second criterion for successful goal setting is to have a "measurement system." Winners always want to know if they're winning or losing. If you don't have a measurement system you can't track your progress. Most people don't have a measurement system for their progress and they end up at the end of the year wondering what happened.

**Examples of measurements:**

| | |
|---|---|
| Number of pounds | Number of prospects |
| Number of people | Number of closes |
| Number of inches | Number of sales, etc. |
| Number of calls | Number of dollars. |

*Time Frame* - The third critical criteria for goal setting is a "time frame." A time frame is essential for a sense of urgency. The sense of urgency creates action. Action is the opposite of procrastination, and procrastination is one of the biggest time wasters. If you've ever watched a professional football game you'll notice that many times the most exciting plays are in the last two minutes of the first half and the last two minutes of the second half.

The reason is the "time frame." The teams know that time is getting short and they have to work harder, smarter, and take more risks.

Also if you don't have any sense of urgency, there's no need to become a master at managing your time.

## *The Next Key Component To Establish Your Goal Is To List <u>All The Benefits</u> You'll Enjoy When You Achieve Your Goal!

You will make decisions and take actions for two reasons. One is a "desire for gain." The other is "fear of loss." The **"fear of loss" is much stronger** than the "desire for gain." For that reason you must make a long list of BENEFITS you'll receive from achieving your goal. If you don't have a long list of benefits for working on your goals plan it'll be tough for you to stay motivated to work on your goals.

**\*The next major step in setting your goal is to identify the obstacles that may come up that will prevent you from achieving your goal.**

Think about this. If there weren't obstacles standing in your way for achieving your goals, wouldn't you already have achieved them? The obstacle could be physical or they could be mental. Most of your obstacles you'll encounter are going to be "MENTAL." In other words most of your obstacles are "**self imposed**."

Remember in chapter two you learned that all of your accomplishments and achievements come from **"what goes into your mind."** The way your mind was programmed will be the major factor to consider when it comes to becoming more successful. If you want to change your success you must change how your mind works.

Your self-esteem and self-image act as a thermostat to regulate your success. If you want to change your success you must change your self-image and self-esteem. The greatest challenge with this is that your self-esteem and self-image are regulated by your "**subconscious mind**." And when you attempt to change you work on your "conscious part of your mind."

A I mentioned earlier, the best resource for changing your subconscious mind is to study the works done by Maxwell Maltz. His best selling book is titled, "Psychocybernetics." If you do nothing more than changing your "Success Mechanism" (How you see yourself in your minds eye) you'll achieve more than if you learn the tricky closes everyone else teaches.

### Self-Esteem—The Main Ingredient For Your Success!

*"Self-Esteem is a life and death issue! Only when you feel respectful of yourself can you be respectful of others and other living things. You can give only what you have, nothing more. Therefore, you love, earn money, communicate, have relationships, manage, teach, sell, parent, nurture and accept differences based only on your Self-Esteem!"* – William J. McGrane

Self-Esteem, as I use the term, is the self-respect you feel for yourself. It is a *feeling*! Psychiatrist and author Carl Jung once said, "We need not pretend to understand the world only by intellect; we apprehend it just as much by *feeling*." Self-Esteem affects all seven areas of your life: Spiritual, Social, Mental, Physical, Financial, Family and Career.

*"You can observe Self-Esteem in the behavior you and others display on a moment-to-moment basis. Please be aware that your Self-Esteem is always fluctuating, it is always in process, it is intangible and it is recognized in your behavior. As a result, you may feel very respectful of yourself one moment, while in the next your Self-Esteem can be in the pits."* – William J. McGrane

**\*List Action Steps Needed To Achieve Your Goals.** After listing the obstacles that will prevent you from achieving your goals you then list the action steps for your plan.

**"If you fail to plan, you're planning to fail."** The action steps are the heart and soul of your goals plan. You have to identify all actions you need to take.

I recall asking Paul Meyer what he meant when he said, *"If you're not making the progress you'd like to make and think you're capable of making, it's simply because you're goals aren't clearly defined."*

I thought he meant I must only have a "specifically" defined goal. But he told me this, ***"You must define the action steps you need to take, the people you need to work with, the skills you need to learn, the resources you need to have available for you, etc."*** When you do that, you'll have a clearly defined goal.

Make a list of action steps you need to take and list them in chronological order they need to be accomplished.

Now you need to make a list of affirmations to read daily when you read your goals. The reasons affirmations are critical is the need to input positive information into your mind. 80% to 90% of everything you're exposed to daily is negative. It's easier for humans to think negatively than it is to think positively. Another word for thinking positively is, "faith." If you think positively, you have faith you're going to succeed.

One way to keep a positive outlook is to read positive, uplifting material. Associate with positive thinking people. And read your affirmations three times a day when you read your goals. This will condition your "subconscious mind" to think "you can" versus thinking "you can't."

## AFFIRMATIONS KEEP YOU IN
## A POSITIVE FRAME OF MIND

I've included a list of affirmations I use. You can pick and choose the ones that you feel most apply to you. Use the whole list if you so choose.

(By the way my definition of an affirmation is as follows: An affirmation is a statement made in the positive, first person, and present tense.)

- I live each day with passion and purpose.

- I am a success in all that I do.

- I respect my abilities and I always fulfill my potential.

- I always have enough money for all that I need.

- My business is now filled with prosperity and abundance.

- I easily achieve all my goals and dreams.

- I am totally confident.

- I am an excellent businessperson.

- I am wealthy and successful, every day, in all that I do.

- I use my wealth and prosperity very wisely.

- I now have all the resources necessary to fulfill any and all of my business goals and dreams.

- Making money excites me and energizes me.

- I am a powerful and resourceful creator.

- I have absolute and certainty in my ability to generate any amount of income I choose.

- I have all the resources I need right now to become a multimillionaire.

- I have great abundance flowing into my business, which affords every luxury that I desire.

- I am an organized, proactive, disciplined, talented, innovative, and intelligent businessperson applying sound and honest business practices.

- I am a powerful and resourceful creator attracting all the wealth and opportunities I need for me to meet my financial success.

- I have all the skills, intelligence, contacts, and money I need right now to create an incredible masterpiece with my business.

- I deserve to earn money easily and in abundance and to live totally paid in full and on time on all accounts. I am completely paid in full on all accounts and money is flowing to me from expected and unexpected sources.

- I deserve happiness, abundance, and prosperity.
- I accomplish my financial goals with ease.
- I have complete freedom over my time.
- I am a genius and I use my wisdom every moment.
- Day by day, in every way, I am better and better.
- I am inquisitive, creative, fun loving, and adventurous.
- I have the extraordinary ability to accomplish everything I choose and want.
- I am committed, determined, and passionate about what I do.
- I am very focused and persistent.
- I have tremendous energy and focus for achieving all my business goals.
- My business is a masterpiece.
- I meditate daily and stay in constant sync with the vibration of abundance and success.
- I visualize all that I desire and I have complete control over manifesting it all.
- I feel happy and at peace with myself.
- I give myself permission to be powerful.
- I have absolute certainty about my ability to generate any amount of income I choose.
- I consistently attract all the right people to help me grow my business.
- I am a brilliant and savvy businessperson.
- I have all the talent, intelligence, and money I need.
- I am a master at what I do.

## "You Must Visualize Yourself Succeeding"

*Visualization-(My definition of Visualization is very close to the word, "vision." Visualize your vision and it'll come to pass. As was said in the Bible, *"If the people have no vision, they shall perish."*)

The last component of a successful goals plan is to practice visualization. When you practice visualization this is another form of meditation. Maxwell Maltz's concept of visualization was practicing going into the "Theatre Of Your Mind." What he means by this is to, "Visualize your past experiences of winning and succeeding and visualize yourself doing the same in the future." This way you program your subconscious to change your "Self-regulating thermostat" for success.

The first step is to remember past successes. Your profession is selling. Now think about some of your biggest sales you've made. If you're just beginning and don't have any big sales to your credit yet, read about successful sales people and visualize you doing what they did. If you're an athlete and you're getting ready to compete, think about all the success you've had in your sport and not the failures.

**The Art Of Visualizing:**

Find a quiet place and get relaxed. You really need to be setting. (When I first started doing this I would lie down to begin my meditation and visualization. The next thing I knew, I was asleep. When I began my visualization by being seated, I was much more successful.) Get relaxed and think about a relaxing place you've been that's very peaceful. Maybe it's by the ocean. Maybe a peaceful stream. When you are relaxed begin seeing yourself becoming successful at whatever you do. If you sell, see yourself closing every deal with no resistance.

If you're getting ready to give a speech visualize everyone congratulating you on an inspiring, outstanding speech. As you continue to do this daily, you'll find your production will greatly improve.

The visualization process is the last part of the goal setting process. Take a day or two at the end of the year and create goals for all areas of your life.

The different areas to concentrate on are:

***Social.** How much you're involved in your community.

***Mental.** How much do you do on a regular basis to sharpen your mind.

***Physical**. Are you in good health, good shape, and looking to live a long, productive life?

***Spiritual.** Are you connecting with your spiritual creator the way you want?

***Financial**. Are you earning the income you "deserve" to earn? Are you investing what you want to invest? Are you saving as much as you'd like to save?

***Family**. Are you spending as much "quality" time with you family you'd like? Are you able to watch your children participate in their sports? Are you able to take vacations with them?

***Career.** Is your career progressing the way you hoped it would? Are you working where you envisioned yourself working? Are you headed in the direction you want your career to move? The more you work and focus on your goals the more they'll work on you.

*"Success is the progressive realization of predetermined, personal, worthwhile goals."*

## Paul J. Meyer

"If we were meeting here three years from today—and you were to look back over those three years to today—what has to have happened during that period, both personally and professionally, for you to feel happy about your progress?"

**List your five most crucial goals you want to accomplish over the next three years.**

1. _____

2. _____

3. _____

4. _____

5. _____

**List why each goal is so important.**

1. _____

2. _____

3. _____

4. _____

5. _____

**What is the truth about your present situation in relation to each goal?**

1. _____

2. _____

3. _____

4. _____

5. _____

**What is the most important action to take for each goal?**

1. _____

2. _____

3. _____

4. _____

5. _____

## One – Year Goals

In the next 12 months my outcomes will be:

**Professional:**

_____

_____

_____

_____

_____

**Personal:**

_____

_____

_____

_____

_____

_____

**90 – day Goals**

List 5 professional goals you will accomplish in the next 90 days:

**Professional Goal:**

(Selling skills, selling activities, financial, management, etc.)

_____

_____

_____

_____

_____

THE ULTIMATE SALES SYSTEM FOR PROFESSIONALS

List 5 personal goals you will accomplish in the next 90 days.

**Personal Goal:**

(physical fitness, family, social, mental, spiritual, etc.)

_____

_____

_____

_____

_____

**Achieving My Goals**

To reach my goals, I will need help from:

(partner, spouse, friend, associate, mentor, resources, etc.)

_____

_____

_____

_____

_____

_____

Other Resources You will need:

_____

_____

_____

_____

_____

# CHAPTER 4
# ACTION IS CRITICAL FOR YOUR SUCCESS

## *"Very Seldom Will You Fail In Selling Because You Have Too Much Good Sales Activity!"*

### David Sims

Another major key for you to succeed in selling is your "Activity." I often make this statement when I'm conducting sales training or speaking to groups about marketing and selling. Here it goes. See if you can find the key part of the statement. *"I've only known one salesperson to go out of business because he made too many calls."* I've made that statement hundreds of times and very few people get it.

Almost all salespeople make too little money because they don't have enough prospects to call on. They just don't have enough activity. Most people in sales are spending too much time getting ready. They may be checking their mail; Or searching the Internet; It could be a multitude of things. You've got to have the right number of prospects plus the right kind of prospects, to call on. That's really a marketing challenge more than it is a sales challenge. Here's what I mean about that.

If you have a poor marketing system, that is a system that brings very few interested prospects either calling or coming to your business, then you end up with the other alternative. What's that alternative you ask? It's one of the most used method of selling. It's "COLD CALLING!" This is the least effective but most common type of marketing used by most sales organizations.

Business owners and sales managers want their sales people to look busy whether they're accomplishing anything or not. They think "cold-calling" is great because they usually haven't done much of it.

Cold calling is very demoralizing to a sales group because this approach results in very few sales, it creates frustration, it produces low incomes, increases rejection, burnout, and turnover. **(One of the best ways to over come that is to have a great referral system in place, like my Ultimate Referral System our company offers.)**

To become successful in selling you must have a minimum of 20 to 25 Grade A prospects in your pipeline at all times. These prospects are somewhere between hello, nice to meet you, to writing a check to you or your company for your product or service. As a general rule these will usually close somewhere between 30 and 90 days.

## What Is The Definition Of A Grade A Prospect?

**(A "Grade A" prospect has three qualities:**

- They have a "NEED" for what you provide.
- They have the "MONEY" to make a purchase or the willingness to make a purchase.
- You can get in front of the "DECISION MAKER" to get a "yes or no."

# Your Sales Pipeline

## "You Need A Continual Pipeline Of Prospects"

What is a "prospect pipeline?" Imagine holding a small piece of pipe in your hand. The pipe could be two or three feet in length and about an inch in diameter. Now you begin stuffing marbles in one end of the pipe. You put one then two then three, etc. Eventually the marbles will begin coming out the other end.

This is the same analogy as a "sales pipeline." You develop a marketing system in which you begin marketing to your "Ideal or Better Than Average" prospects. You continually market to your "pipeline of prospects" until they get ready to buy.

You must continue to put prospects in your pipeline. Remember the pipe and marble example. As long as you continue to put marbles in one end, they'll come out the other end. Your prospect pipeline is the same. If you stop marketing or stop putting prospects in your pipeline, soon your sales will dry up.

If you have 100 prospects in your pipeline and one deal goes sour on you it's no big deal. However, if you only have four prospects in your pipeline and one goes sour then you have a real problem.

Remember, seldom will you fail because you have to much activity. (I.e. too many sales interviews.) If you fail it'll be because you don't have enough activity with the right kind of prospects.

# Sales Pipeline – Top 20 Club

(Add prospects to your list each month.)
Your top 20 club are your prospects you work to close in the next 30 to 90 days.

| Name | Address | Telephone # | E-mail | Website |
|------|---------|-------------|--------|---------|
| 1 | | | | |
| 2 | | | | |
| 3 | | | | |
| 4 | | | | |
| 5 | | | | |
| 6 | | | | |
| 7 | | | | |
| 8 | | | | |
| 9 | | | | |
| 10 | | | | |
| 11 | | | | |
| 12 | | | | |
| 13 | | | | |
| Etc. | | | | |

# What Feeds Your Sales Pipeline?
# Your Farm Club

**(Potential clients in Future – Your goal is to cultivate this list and move them to your pipeline within the next 90-180 days or sooner)**

The second Pipeline you want in place is called, "Your Farm Club." In your farm club you want 20 to 25 prospects you don't know much about but you'll find out more about them and begin marketing to them. Your goal is to develop a relationship with them and move them into your Sales Pipe Line. They are the same Class A type companies or individuals you need to grow your business. You put the list together and you're begin working on them 90 to 180 days out before you try to sell them.

You need to develop a marketing plan to keep yourself in front of them on a weekly or monthly basis. You send them a handwritten, personal note. You send them an article of interest to them. Or you create the occasion for you to meet them personally if you can. You do something to keep your name in front of them monthly or more regularly.

# Your Farm Club

| | Name | $ | Phone # | Best Results To Date | Next Step |
|---|---|---|---|---|---|
| 1. | | | | | |
| 2. | | | | | |
| 3. | | | | | |
| 4. | | | | | |
| 5. | | | | | |
| 6. | | | | | |
| 7. | | | | | |
| 8. | | | | | |
| 9. | | | | | |
| 10. | | | | | |
| 11. | | | | | |
| 12. | | | | | |
| 13. | | | | | |
| 14. | | | | | |
| 15. | | | | | |
| 16. | | | | | |
| 17. | | | | | |
| 18. | | | | | |
| 19. | | | | | |
| 20. | | | | | |

# CHAPTER 5
# IF YOU CAN'T MEASURE IT, YOU CAN'T MANAGE IT!

If you want to become more successful, one of the rules to follow is this, **"What gets measured always improves."** All winners always want to know if they're winning or losing. The best way to do that is to measure your daily activity. However, not only is it important to measure you must know the Key Function Indicators you need to measure.

A Key Function Indicator (KFI) is an activity that directly affects outcomes. When I first started selling there were certain activities I measured that had a direct impact on my productivity.

The three Key Function Indicators you need to measure that have a direct bearing on your success are these:

1. Face-to-Face-Interviews. The number of in person sales interviews you have with decision makers.

2. The number of phone calls you make to schedule appointments. (In reality this is the only part of the sales process you can control.)

3. The number of Class A prospects you add to your pipeline each week.

## What One Action Can You Take
## That Will Accelerate Your Success?

I've created a "success journal" for you. All you have to do is to copy it and keep it with you when you go on sales calls. The topics to track in your journal are critical for your sales skills development.

After every face-to-face interview you conduct, immediately log the results into your journal. The remarkable common thread you'll find is this, *"If you make a sale it will probably be because you did a great job of uncovering prospects pain, in the pain step. If you didn't make a sale or schedule a follow up meeting, it was because you didn't do a thorough job in the pain step."*

I suggest you photocopy the Success Journal and fill it out after each sales call you make. You'll find the better you are at uncovering **pain** the easier it is to sell. Here's the key, **if you can't uncover any of the prospects pain, you can't sell them.** You'll then revert to the strategy most salespeople use, **"You'll try to make the sale by being the lowest bidder."** That's a terrible way to try to build a business. Especially because **the lowest bidder always goes out of business!**

## <u>Success Journal</u>

Date:_____ Time:_____

Appointment with _____ of _____
                         (name)                       (company)

Contact information_____.

1. What was the best result obtained from my meeting?

_____

_____

2. What different outcome could have been produced that would have been a plus?

_____

_____

3. What 3 needs (pains) did I uncover?

A. _____

B. _____

C. _____

4. Do they have a budget for my product or service? If so, how much? If not, where will they get the money?

_____

_____

5. Was the person I met with the decision maker? If the person is not the decision maker, who is the decision maker and what is their process?

_____

_____

6. What's the next step?

_____

_____

(If you didn't make the sale, obtaining a "next step" is critical. If you come away from the meeting with a "next step" you are still in the selling process and your chances of making the sale continue to rise.)

# <u>Success Journal</u>

Date:_____ Time:_____

Appointment with _____ of _____
      (name)                    (company)

Contact information_____.

1. What was the best result obtained from my meeting?

_____

_____

2. What different outcome could have been produced that would have been a plus?

_____

_____

3. What 3 needs (pains) did I uncover?

   A. _____

   B. _____

   C. _____

4. Do they have a budget for my product or service? If so, how much? If not, where will they get the money?

_____

_____

5. Was the person I met with the decision maker? If the person is not the decision maker, who is the decision maker and what is their process?

_____

_____

6. What's the next step?

_____

_____

(If you didn't make the sale, obtaining a "next step" is critical. If you come away from the meeting with a "next step" you are still in the selling process and your chances of making the sale continue to rise.)

## <u>Success Journal</u>

Date:_____ Time:_____

Appointment with _____ of _____
                        (name)                    (company)

Contact information_____.

1. What was the best result obtained from my meeting?

_____

_____

2. What different outcome could have been produced that would have been a plus?

_____

_____

3. What 3 needs (pains) did I uncover?

    A. _____

    B. _____

    C. _____

4. Do they have a budget for my product or service? If so, how much? If not, where will they get the money?

_____

_____

5. Was the person I met with the decision maker? If the person is not the decision maker, who is the decision maker and what is their process?

_____

_____

6. What's the next step?

_____

_____

(If you didn't make the sale, obtaining a "next step" is critical. If you come away from the meeting with a "next step" you are still in the selling process and your chances of making the sale continue to rise.)

DAVID L. SIMS

# CHAPTER 6
# THE TEN TRUTHS ABOUT SELLING YOU SHOULD KNOW

Attitude-

*"The posture or position of a person showing or meant to show a mental state, emotion, or mood."*

*"The manner of acting, feeling, or thinking that shows one's disposition, opinion, etc." –*
Webster

I want you to visualize a triangle. This will be your "Sales Success Triangle." There are three components making up your "Sales Success Triangle." The first point is going to be the most important one. We'll label the top point "Attitude."

Your "Attitude" point will consist of three components. The first component is "your attitude about yourself." How do you feel about yourself? Do you feel that you deserve to be successful? Do you feel self-confident? Do feel like a winner? Do you like yourself? Do you have a "high self-esteem? Do you have a healthy "self-image" of your self?

The second component of your "**Attitude**" point is how you feel about the company you represent. Do you like your company? Do you think your company has a good product? Do you like the people in your company? Do you think they provide a better product and service than anyone else?

The third component of your "Attitude" point is how you feel about your marketplace. Do you like the city you cover? Do you enjoy selling and servicing in your marketplace. Do you feel your marketplace is as good or better than others?

Here's a key for you to recognize. Your "Attitude" about yourself will comprise about 80% of the "Attitude" point. So you must do everything possible to build your attitude up each and every day.

The second point of your "Sales Success Triangle" is your "Behavior". Your behavior is defined by the habits you've formed over the years. Do you make calls on a regular basis? Do you take stalls, objections, and put-off's easily? Or do you just see the stalls, put-offs and objections as a signal to sell more? Do you use your time wisely?

There are only about three activities that will really make you money when it comes to selling.

1.  Face-to-face interviews.

2.  Prospecting.

3.  Calling to schedule appointments with decision-makers.

If you're engaged in activities other than those three you are not making good use of your time. I do my calling, prospecting, and interviews between 8:00am and 5:00pm. All of my other activities like planning, research, bookkeeping, etc. I do at other times of the day or on weekends. You probably remember the Success Pathway listed in a previous chapter. In that I described where your behavior fit into your success.

The final component of your "Sales Success Triangle" is your Knowledge point. How well do you know your product and service? Product knowledge and Behavior make up about 20% of the "Sales Success Triangle." If you feel you can sell effectively because you have a lot of product knowledge you'll be selling at a disadvantage.

When I hire sales people for companies I find it's easier to hire a sales person and teach them product knowledge than it is to hire a "technician" and try to teach them about sales. The thing about being technically oriented is that "too much product knowledge" can bore a prospect to tears. Remember, one of the ways people feel uncomfortable is to talk in language they don't understand. I.e. too much product knowledge.

## Do You Evaluate Your Behavior?

Would you like to play a Self-Esteem "true or false" game? Write your answers of "true" or "false" to each statement on a piece of paper.

1. I had intact Self-Esteem when I was born.
2. My present Self-Esteem was created by significant others in my life.
3. My present attitudes are affirming or not affirming based on the role models in my life.
4. The definition of Self-Esteem is the way I *feel* about myself.
5. My ability to describe my feelings helps me to reduce tension and distress.
6. My ability to listen to others is an indication of my Self-Esteem.
7. Finality Statements kill Self-Esteem communication.
8. Finishing sentences for other is unintact Self-Esteem behavior.
9. Interrupting others is a sign of not intact Self-Esteem.
10. Criticizing others shows not intact Self-Esteem.
11. Putting people down displays not intact Self-Esteem choice.
12. Name-calling demonstrates "not intact" Self-Esteem.
13. Labeling other people is not intact Self-Esteem behavior.
14. Comparing yourself with others harms your Self-Esteem.
15. Trying to prove yourself to other people is a sign of not intact Self-Esteem.

16. Avoiding responsibility for everything you think, say, do, or *feel* is not intact Self-Esteem behavior.

17. Getting drunk displays not intact Self-Esteem behavior.

18. Dependency on drugs is a sign of not intact Self-Esteem.

19. Depending on others for you to *feel* good displays low Self-Esteem

20. Choosing to be healthy is an intact Self-Esteem choice.

21. Choosing to be sick is an un-intact Self-Esteem choice.

22. Shyness is a sign of un-intact Self-Esteem.

23. Depressing *feelings* is a sign of un-intact Self-Esteem.

24. Enthusiasm and a zest for life is intact Self-Esteem behavior.

25. Overeating is un-intact Self-Esteem behavior.

26. Obesity and being overweight is un-intact Self-Esteem behavior.

27. Procrastination shows un-intact Self-Esteem.

28. Inability to make decisions is un-intact Self-Esteem behavior.

29. Building and maintaining relationships is a sign of intact Self-Esteem.

30. Releasing your full potential is intact Self-Esteem behavior.

31. Holding grudges in un-intact Self-Esteem behavior.

32. Fear of speaking in groups is a sign of un-intact Self-Esteem.

33. Career unhappiness reflects un-intact Self-Esteem.

34. Complimenting people is intact Self-Esteem behavior.

35. Creating an affirming lifestyle is intact Self-Esteem behavior.

36. Giving recognition to others is intact Self-Esteem behavior.

(Your answers should all be "yes." If the majority of your answers are "no" then you have a need to do some work on your self-esteem.)

## 10 Activities To Have A High-Energy Day

1. Release criticizing yourself and others.

2. Release comparing yourself with others.

3.  Release getting angry and resentful.

4.  Release blaming anyone for anything.

5.  Release working or living in a toxic environment.

6.  Start giving Self-Esteem messages to everyone.

7.  Start giving compliments to everyone.

8.  Start an exercise program and learn to relax.

9.  Start a nutritional eating program.

10. Start learning new skills daily.

# Daily Success Actions

I will work on these three areas this week to develop my attitude.

1.  _____

    _____

    _____

2.  _____

    _____

    _____

3.  _____

    _____

    _____

I will work on these three areas this week to develop my self-esteem.

1.  _____

    _____

_____

2. _____

_____

_____

3. _____

_____

_____

I will list these affirmations on a 3x5 index card and read them three times a day.

1. _____

2. _____

3. _____

4. _____

5. _____

6. _____

7. _____

8. _____

9. _____


10. _____

DAVID L. SIMS

# CHAPTER 7
# HOW TO DOUBLE THE NUMBER OF APPOINTMENTS YOU SET WITH HALF THE EFFORT.

The first step after finding a prospect is to get an appointment to tell your story. The way you are introduced to the prospect dramatically affects your positioning with the prospect in the sales process.

If you are calling cold your chances of gaining an appointment are very, very slim. Depending on the level of client you are calling, your odds can sometimes be as slim as 50 to 1. Besides when you are cold calling you are positioned in the sales process from a position of "weakness." Why is it a position of weakness? It's because you're chasing the prospect instead of him/her chasing you. (If you are referred you are working from a position of strength.) In other words, they are chasing you.

---

**NOTE:** The goal of your contact, (telephone or in person), is only one thing. *You want to schedule an appointment to tell your story in a favorable condition with giving as little information as possible about you or what you do.* As you'll learn in later sessions about communication, it's very difficult to read body language via the telephone.

---

People are busier than ever. They are having to produce more with fewer people. They are constantly bombarded with all sorts of information. What this means to you is that prospects need to have the conviction that your story is compelling enough to capture their attention. Just remember to give as little information as possible to get the appointment. This doesn't mean to be evasive and try to side step the questions the prospect will ask.

The first step to design an effective system for getting appointments is to identify the possible stalls, objections, or put-offs a prospect might bring up for not seeing you.

There are about three reasons someone will buy from you.

1. They like you.
2. They trust you.

3. You can provide a better service, product or value than they are currently getting or you can save them money or make them money.

Usually the sequence goes in that order. Prospects want to get know you and like you. (This is called building relationships.) Then they develop trust in you. And at that time they start to seriously consider if you can solve problems for them.

First you have to get into a favorable meeting to begin the process. Let's look at some techniques for obtaining an appointment.

Let's assume there are three objections that prospects might have for not wanting to schedule an appointment with you.

## Objections

1. Money-They haven't put any money in the budget or they don't want to invest any money with you.
2. Time-The prospect already has more on their plate than they can handle. Now you've asked them to take valuable time out of their day to meet with you and they don't want to.
3. Effort-The prospect is comfortable with their system or product already in place. Subconsciously they are thinking they can endure their current situation easier than they can go through the pain of switching. With the change to you they will have down time, have

installation or implementation challenges. Their routine will be disrupted, etc.

So we're going to design our appointment communication around the three objections of **Time**, **Effort**, and **Money**.

I will describe different scenarios for scheduling appointments.

# Telephone Call—

**You**: Good morning, I'd like to speak to Bob Jones.

**Receptionist**: Just a moment, I'll put you through.

**Bob Jones**: This is Bob Jones.

**You**: Good morning Bob. My name is Don Smith with ABC Company. We help companies like yours increase their profits and productivity. The reason for my call is to schedule a few minutes with you to introduce myself and my company. In the process I'd like to find out a little more about your company. We may be able to provide a service for you, but if we can't you'll know about us should the need ever arise. Is that fair enough?

**Bob Jones**: O.K.

**You**: Which would be better for you, 10:00 a.m. on Tuesday or 2:00 p.m. Wednesday?

**Bob Jones**: How much time do you need?

**You**: About 30 or 45 minutes if we're not interrupted.

**Bob Jones**: O.K.

**You**: I have 2:00 p.m. open on Tuesday afternoon or 10:00 on Wednesday morning. Which of those times are best for you?

**You**: Hello, I'd need to speak with Bob Jones.

**Bob Jones**: This is Bob Jones.

**You**: Present your introduction.

**Bob Jones**: Thanks for calling but we're already using company XYZ.

**You**: I certainly understand that. I'm familiar with XYZ. They're a good company. I understand how you feel. I'm not asking you to make a commitment or to change. One thing we've found with many of our current customers is that they were in the same boat as you when we first met. But here's what they found. We have such a wide spectrum of services that we were able to provide two or three services they weren't receiving.

I have a few minutes open on Monday afternoon at 2:30 p.m. or Thursday morning at 10:30 a.m. which of those times would be best for you?

**Bob Jones**: How much time do you need?

**You**: Our initial meeting is just for introductions and a few brief questions. If I'm there more than 10 minutes it's because you've asked me to stay. (The key to making this work is to remind the prospect at the beginning of the meeting you agreed to only 10 minutes. When 10 minutes has passed in the meeting, you check to see if the prospect wants to continue with the conversation or schedule another meeting. The key is to begin asking questions of your prospect instead of talking about you or your product.)

Is morning or afternoon better for you?

**Bob Jones**: I appreciate your call, but we've already spent all the money we had budgeted for your kind of service.

**You**: Bob, that's not unusual. Many of our clients had the same challenge when we first met. Do you mind if I ask you a question? When is your year end?

**Bob**: December 31st.

**You**: Bob, can I make a suggestion? Let me drop by for a few minutes and introduce myself. I can give you a little information about our company. Maybe ask a couple of questions. Then a couple of months before the end of the year we can connect again and possibly get together again. Is that fair enough?

**Bob**: O.K.

**You**: Bob, which is best for you? I have some time available Wednesday afternoon at 1:15 p.m. or Friday morning at 10:45 a.m.

Should a prospect raise an issue about scheduling, answer it and then ask for an appointment.

---

**NOTE:** When it comes to scheduling appointments the difference between salespeople who succeed and those who fail is the number of times of hearing "NO." The failures quit trying after they hear the "first NO." The successful salespeople continue until they receive 5 or 10 answers of "NO" before they give up.

---

# Set Yourself Apart With A Killer Introduction

A well thought out introduction is critical for breaking the preoccupation barrier of the prospect. Your prospects are continually barraged with your competition, challenges with running their companies, noise in the marketplace, etc. The last thing they are thinking of is you or me calling on them because they have their desk piled high with projects, crisis and people challenges. The list is endless.

You want to break their preoccupation barrier and the best way to do that is with a strong introduction. A strong introduction is needed to get them to stop what they're doing and listen to you. If you don't, 5 minutes after you've called on your prospect, chances are they can't even remember your name.

**NOTE:** Introduce yourself in a way that is clear, concise, and personable, and that generates interest.

You've probably heard the expression, "You never get a second chance to make a first impression."

One of your greatest assets can be a self-introduction that develops relationship and rapport while generating interest.

# Criteria for a Powerful Self-Introduction

**Clear**
Be sure to let people know what you do. You want people to be intrigued but not confused.

**Concise**
Follow the KISS rule (Keep It Short and Simple). Develop an introduction that says what you want to say in seven to ten seconds. The "seven-second syndrome" indicates that the first impression happens in the first seven seconds of meeting someone.

**Distinctive**
Be catchy enough to distinguish yourself from everyone else while also being professional. You can do this by telling people through your introduction what you love about what you do, what your commitment is to you clients, or what is special about the way you do business.

**Relatable**
Use common words (rather than buzzwords or technical terms) and examples that people can relate to so that you immediately develop relationship and rapport.

**Engaging**
Your words, mannerisms, tone of voice, and eye contact can all contribute to people being intrigued, interested, and drawn to you. They will tend to remember your warmth, smile, interest, and enthusiasm.

# <u>Examples</u>

**Vague/Bland:**

>    1. "Hello, my name is David Sims; trainer and public speaker."

**More specific and energetic:**

>    2. "Hello, my name is David Sims, owner of the David Sims Company.  I can teach you to get referrals anywhere and everywhere with everyone you meet to get whatever you want."

**More specific and memorable:**

>    "Hello, my name is David Sims.  I teach referral prospecting as a way to build your business and enhance your life."

**Vague:**

>    1. "Hello, my name is Sue Smith optometrist."

**Specific:**

>    2. "Hello, my name is Sue Smith and I help keep the world in focus.  I'm an optometrist."

**Vague:**

>    1. "Hello, my name is Bob Jones, realtor."

**Specific:**

>    2. "Hello, my name if Bob Jones.  I help people achieve the American Dream, home ownership.  I sell everything from condos to

>    castles."

# Action Steps For This Week

1.  My introduction for myself and my company is _____

    _____

    _____

2.  The three most common objections I hear when attempting to schedule appointments are:

    A.  Objection _____

    _____

    Rebuttal _____

    _____

    B.  Objection _____

    _____

    Rebuttal _____

    _____

    C.  Objection _____

    _____

Rebuttal _____

_____

D.  Objection _____

_____

Rebuttal _____

_____

3.  Additional action steps for this week.

_____

_____

_____

_____

_____

_____

_____

# CHAPTER 8
# DEVELOPING RAPPORT
# TO SELL TO DIFFERENT PERSONALITIES.

| Understanding Social Style Behavior |
|---|

| |
|---|
| There is no right or wrong place to be, it is simply an appraisal matrix used to better understand customers' buying needs. |

| |
|---|
| We must know where we are in order to adapt to our customers' individual needs. |

| |
|---|
| No longer is it enough to be able to sell. To truly succeed you have to know what you are doing and why it is necessary. |

| |
|---|
| Does your sales approach have the same effect on every prospect? |

| |
|---|
| Is it easier to sell some prospects than others? |

| |
|---|
| Have you had a difficult time with a particular type of prospect? |

# Assertiveness

*"Effort Put Forth to Influence Action"*

| Less | D | C | B | A | More |

Less
Assertive
(Asking)

Assertive
(Telling)

**Less Assertive Tend To:**

(C & D)

*Be Patient Decision Makers

*Attentive and Cooperative

*Avoid Wrong Decision and Risks

*Laid Back and Calm

*Calm & Sometimes Demure

*Limits Use of Pressure

*Shows Interest

*Slow Paced

*Listens Well

*Withholds Opinions

*Somewhat Introverted

*Asks Questions

*Goes Along

**More Assertive Tend To:**

(A & B)

*Quick To Take Action

*Competitive and Challenging

*Take Chances

*Leans Forward & Participates

*Uses Emphasis & Inflection

*Presses For Appeal

*Short Attention Span

*Definite Agenda

*Impatient

*Free With Opinions

*Extraverted and Outgoing

*Makes Statements

*Takes Charge

In which of the four sections of the Assertiveness line do you see yourself?

Enter an A, B, C, or D in the rectangle

## Assertiveness Behavior

| Ask-Assertive | Tell-Assertive |
| --- | --- |
| **Voice:**<br><br>Speaks Slowly<br>Pauses Often<br>Is not Intense Speaker<br>Low Sound Level<br>Soft Spoken<br>Has a Questioning Tone | **Voice:**<br><br>Speaks Continuously<br>Fast Paced Pattern<br>Sometimes Becomes Loud<br>Emphatic<br>Has Tone of Certainty<br>Strong Modulation |
| **Body Language:**<br><br>Restrained<br>Gestures are Smooth<br>Movement Gentle<br>Observant<br>Attentive<br>Follows Others Movement | **Body Language:**<br><br>Emphatic with Gestures<br>Uses Props for Clarity<br>Quick Pronounced Movements<br>Leads in Positioning<br>Sometimes Wonders |
| **Statement:**<br><br>Asks Questions<br>Seldom Makes Statements | **Statement:**<br><br>Makes Statements and<br>Prompts |
| **Responsive** | |
| Nervous as Tension Rises<br>Needs Appreciation<br>Low Risk Taker | Sets Requirements Readily<br>Is Direct and Decisive<br>Controls the Conversation |

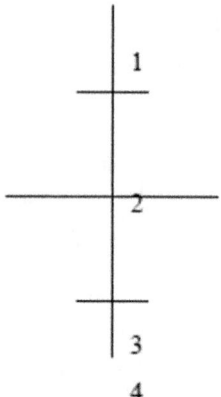

More Responsive

(Emotes Feelings)

| Less Responsive Tend To: | More Responsive Tend To: |
|---|---|
| *Rely on Facts | *Swayed By Emotions |
| *Are Very Controlled | *Openly Displays Feelings |
| *Uses Little or No Body Language | *Uses gestures & Expressions |
| *Sometimes Distant & Cool | *Warm & Friendly |
| *Poker Faced | *Smiles & Frowns |
| *Needs Facts & Reasons | *Needs Opinions & Feelings |
| *Calm & Calculating | *Excitable |
| *Has Definite Time Restraints | *Time is Flexible |
| *Serious | *Friendly |
| *Disciplined | *Spontaneous |

In which of the four sections of the Responsive Line do you see Yourself?

Enter a 1, 2, 3, or 4 in the rectangle

# Responsive Behavior

| Emote-Responsive | Control-Responsive |
|---|---|
| **Voice:** | **Voice:** |
| Speaks With Dimension<br>Has Range of Voice Inflection<br>Varies Tone<br>Alternates Approach in<br>    Speaking | Deliberate<br>Formal<br>No Range of Tone<br>Limited Expression |
| **Body Language:** | **Body Language:** |
| Spontaneous Use of Body<br>Many Facial Expressions<br>Good Eye Contact<br>Hands Open and Moving | Careful<br>Controlled<br>Indirect Eye Contact<br>Limited Gestures<br>Hands Closed |
| **Statement:** | **Statement:** |
| Shares Personal Feelings<br>Enthusiastic to Benefits<br>Uses Intuition<br>Wants Collaboration<br>Emphatic | Noncommittal<br>Conceals Personal Feelings<br>Relies on Facts<br>Wants Response<br>Measured objectivity<br>Limited Immediate Response |

## The Social Style Matrix

Less Responsive (Controls)

| D1 | C1 | B1 | A1 |
|---|---|---|---|
| Analytical | Analytical-Driver | Driver-Analytical | Driver-Driver |
| **D2** | **C2** | **B2** | **A2** |
| Analytical-Amiable | Analytical-Expressive | Driver-Amiable | Driver-Expressive |
| **D3** | **C3** | **B3** | **A3** |
| Amiable-Analytical | Amiable-Driver | Expressive-Analytical | Expressive-Driver |
| **D4** | **C4** | **B4** | **A4** |
| Amiable-Amiable | Amiable-Expressive | Expressive-Amiable | Expressive-Expressive |

Less Assertive (Asks) ← → More Assertive (Tells)

More Responsive (Emotes)

| Analytical (Avoiding) | Driver (Autocratic) |
|---|---|
| Amiable (Acquiesing) | Expressive (Attacking) |

Each quadrant repeats itself within the other. The deeper you learn to appraise the better you will be able to serve the needs of your client.

# Drivers

Are goal-oriented people who focus on results. Many drivers are workaholics and are taskmasters who want to get things done and move on to the next project. He or she measures success by achievements. Drivers are decisive people who are quick to take action but will compete for the best deal. They have a short attention span and are willing to take calculated risks.

As buyers they are concerned about the bottom line and want to get to it quickly. Drivers do not want any small talk, you must first win their respect and confidence. They have a low tolerance for feelings, attitudes and unqualified advice of others.

**To Adapt:**

You should present yourself in a businesslike manner and get to the point quickly. Introduce yourself and listen intently to his concerns offering your support of his concerns. Explain in brief detail of your mission and confirm his expectations. Focus complete attention on his agenda, ideas and priorities. Let your personality show with some reserve, always keeping close to business formality.

Be factual in presentation targeted to his needs and provide evidence to support your facts. Ask fact-finding questions which will lead to the Drivers main concerns and what has value to him. Your questions must be consistent to his objectives and reveal his priorities. Your recommendations should include alternative options and their benefits or adverse effects

explained. Your offer should be of the very best quality within the Driver's budget limits. Do not overwhelm with details; appeal to his self-esteem and reinforce his openness and honesty in the interview. Summarize your offers and let him choose a course of action.

Ask for the order directly, including options and alternatives, then be prepared to negotiate changes and concessions with him. Many Drivers will attach conditions to the sale. Anticipate his objections and be prepared with documented facts and testimonials. His first objection is seldom his real objection and you must do some probing to get at his underlying concern. Do not pop any surprises on the Driver after the proposal is completed or there will be hell to pay. The entire process should be fast paced and to the point.

# Analyticals

Are very cautious decision makers, who thrive on structure and organization. They will ask a lot of questions and will surprise you at their knowledge of the industry and product offering. Analyticals are good problem solvers and work well alone, being very precise in all that they do. They are often slow paced and articulate in details. They are viewed as laid back, somewhat boring and always picky about small details. They have a good technical mind and love lots of factual data. Analyticals are more task oriented and can dispense with building a personal relationship and engaging is small talk. They want to be always right in all that they do, hence they tend to over-rely on data collected.

**To Adapt:**

Present yourself in a professional manner and bring lots of product and service data (he will read it all). Provide details about yourself and your company because he will consider everything in his decision-making. You should simply become an ADVISOR to the Analytical do to his expert research prior to your visit. The Analytical, like the Driver, has his own agenda and his time is important to him.

Provide testimonies and evidence your solution will and has worked for third party clients. Your questions must be well organized, specific and systematic. Factual information should be in balance with his ideas and feelings. He will naturally tell you more than you will want to know and that will help you when it comes time to close and answer his objections. Your demeanor should be reserved but not cool and you must be decisive without seeming too aggressive. Be specific in your proposal and stand fast. Do not appeal to his emotions they are deep seated.

Ask for the order directly, in a low-keyed manner. Be prepared to negotiate on several details. He will probably push for an itemized price breakdown of the total job. Zero in on his commitment for urgency. Keep the interview moving at his pace.

# Amiables

Are patient in taking action or making a decision. They need to establish close personal relationships and feel comfortable with you. Amiables are good listeners, have a pleasing personality and want to know others' feelings on a particular matter. They have a difficult time with goal setting and self-direction. They are low risk takers in all that they do. They do not get mad now, they get even later. They will cooperate and offer information and feelings on their needs, which are often understated. They will disguise budget concerns and value justifications on the surface. They may put you off with needing additional help in making a decision.

**To Adapt:**

Continually confirm the Amiables understanding and feelings on topics of discussion. Reinforce their assurance you can solve their problems, in their best interest. Use references known to the Amiable, either personally or by position. Take your time with Amiables and be prepared to talk about anything and everything. Take your sleeping bag and photo albums. Be sure to cover all the soft bases in your proposal (safety, comfort, savings and conservation etc.). Key in on warranties and personal care.

When trying to close, ask for the order indirectly, without pressure. Do not work them into a corner with no way out. Instill you personal involvement and your follow-up process. Be ready for buyer's remorse to set in if you can not react immediately to their order. Answer objections patiently and compliment the interest shown. Finance programs are important to Amiables and could sway their decision. Constantly reassure them they have made the right decision and will not regret it in the future. Do not hurry the Amiable; they need to take their time and get to know you. The way they feel about you is just as important as buying the right system.

## Expressives

Are "let's get it done" people full of enthusiasm and excitement. They love to talk and stimulate the conversation beyond necessity. They talk with their whole body at times, using facial expressions, hands, voice inflection and credentials early on. A professional business manner should be projected and you must earn the Expressive's right to do business with him. Be enthusiastic about his ideas and concerns.

Share perceived exclusive information with him. Get his feelings on what he expects his ideal outcome to be. Key in on using stories and relationships you both have in common. Build his competence in your confidence and develop the relationship on a personal and open basis. Ask fact-finding questions that will reveal his needs, wants and hot buttons. He wants your opinions and personal feelings on all issues concerning his investment. They are not much concerned with details and fine tuning the total package, they want to know they can trust you, but be results oriented. Do not overwhelm them with details or you will loose them in the process. Do not rush the sales interview, their time is flexible; try to appeal to their self-esteem needs and get his commitment.

**To Adapt:**

Always assume the sale with Expressives and ask for the order in a very casual manner. They will always be enticed by price breaks, small concessions, value added ancillary products or some type of incentive. Once you have gotten his commitment, be sure in a casual way, he understands his decision to buy.

Do not burden him with the details; he feels that is your job. When dealing with his objections, restate his benefits, remind him of his wants and needs stated by him, and relate how others have handled the hesitation hi is faced with. You have a friend for life so get used to it and stay in touch. The Expressive will pass many referrals your way and their testimonial is invaluable. Take your time and concentrate on the prospect and not the product.

## What It All Means To You

Learning how to appraise Social Style Behavior will take some practice and patients to become good at it. The deeper you can appraise, the better you will get at it.

Now that you know your Social Style Behavior, you will become better at adapting to the needs of your prospects. Learning how to relate and communicate in the way our customers are most comfortable will give us the competitive edge in the sales arena. Our prospective buyers have the same reservations and emotions about us, prior to a sales call, as we do them.

This appraisal is our only clue to how the prospect prefers to do business. We do not have the luxury of knowing the buyer's thoughts because they are concealed in his mind, we really can not tell what his true feelings are on a matter unless he shares them with us. All we can really bank on is what the prospect says and does or how he relates his needs through words and body language. People tend to behave in established, observable patterns. It is difficult to hide these patterns of behavior.

In given situations, the behavior patterns you are able to observe are the behavior patterns you must use to form your appraisal of the prospect and use to plan your sales interview.

Customers would rather buy from you than be sold. They want to buy, the way they like to buy. No longer is "single style of selling" relevant in today's customer driven marketplace. Instead, building strong interpersonal relationships and buyer trust is mandatory. We must accommodate our buyers by altering our own habitual behavior patterns to serve the prospect's needs. Our behavior must complement the buyer's buying behavior.

# CHAPTER 9
# NINE STEPS TO CREATE CREDIBILITY IN THE SALES PROCESS

## Steps to building credibility for you and your company

Building credibility for you or your company is critical. People will do business with you for three reasons:

1. They like you.
2. They trust you.
3. You provide a better value, product, or service. Also you help them either earn money or save money.

The key in the formula is number 2. They must **trust you**. There is a "TRUST GAP" between you and your prospect. Imagine you standing on one side of a canyon and your prospect standing on the other side. The canyon represents the **TRUST GAP**. The idea here is that you and the prospect need to be on the same side of the canyon (close the trust gap) before you'll do business with them. The less the prospect knows about you, the wider the gap. The quickest way to close the "TRUST GAP" is to get a referral to your prospect from someone having influence with them. You then have instant credibility. If you're not referred to a prospect you then must do every thing possible to build credibility.

1. The quickest way to build credibility is to have someone refer you to the prospect. The person referring you must have influence with the prospect. When you are referred a critical part of your success is to have the person referring you introduce you to the prospect before you attempt to schedule an appointment.

2. Another method to build credibility is to present articles published about you or your company.

3. Have client comments available for the prospect. The comments should include benefits of working with you and your company.

4. Have testimonial letters written to you by enthusiastic clients.

5. List awards presented to you or your company for outstanding service or contributions.

6. List charities or other non-profits you've served.

7. Write a book about your field. Being an author is a great credibility creator.

8. Become a public speaker. Most people believe if you can speak before a group you are credible.

# CHAPTER 10
# THE KEY TO EFFECTIVE SELLING IS DEVELOP THE SKILLS TO ASK EFFECTIVE, COMPELLING QUESTIONS.

During the entire sales process your degree of success will depend upon your ability to ask compelling, effective questions.

Before beginning the steps to the process we must establish some "Caution" points.

**Caution**
You must know the answer you want before you design the question.

**Caution**
To get information you must give information.

**Caution**
In preparation for a question you must "nurture, nurture, nurture."
(You may have heard the saying about retail sales: "The key to success is location, location, location." In the development of your skills to ask questions the key to   success is nurture, nurture, nurture.)

**Caution**
Use softening statements before asking a question.

**Caution**
Avoid using technical buzz words during your sales call.  Your prospect or customer may not understand and this could make them feel not o.k. about themselves.

**Caution**

Don't become emotionally involved. The prospect can become emotionally involved but you must remove your emotions from the situation. Prospects make buying decisions emotionally and they justify their decision logically or intellectually.

**Caution**

When first meeting a prospect and they ask you questions such as:

- Can you solve our problem?

- How much will it cost for you to work with us?

- What can you do for us? etc.

Your response always is, **"I don't know."** The reason being you have to assess their situation before you propose a solution.

**Caution**

Sell before you educate. Many salespeople give a lot of free consulting away.

The essential ingredient for becoming successful in the sales field or building relationships is the ability to become an effective communicator. Communication is divided into these components.

- Verbal        _____7_%
- Tonal        _____38_____ %
- Non-Verbal        _____55_____ %

The three components combine to form 100% of your communication skill. What percentage does each component comprise?

# VERBAL COMMUNICATION

**Verbal communication refers to the words you use during your conversation**.

Questions to ask yourself about your verbal communication skills.

- Am I using words prospects or customers don't understand?
- Am I speaking at a rate similar to my prospect or customer?
- Do I sabotage my communication by using subtalk instead of power language?
  ex.: subtalk-maybe, if, I'll try, etc.

- Are my questions and answers well thought out and spoken clear and concise?
- Do I answer questions too quickly?
- Do I use a tape recorder to tape my presentations, interviews, or attempt to obtain appointments? Then review the recordings and study them to make improvements?

The three action steps I will take this week to develop my verbal communication skills are:

1. _____

   _____

2. _____

   _____

3. _____

   _____

## Tonal Communication

Tonal communication refers to the tone of voice you use when speaking. Do you remember the adage, "it's not what you say but how you say it?" This is true of "Tonal Communication."

Some questions to ask yourself about your "Tonal Communication."

Am I insincere in my conversation?

- Am I condescending?
- Is my tone high pitched?
- Is my tone irregular?
- Is my tone nurturing and non-threatening?

# Non-Verbal Communication

Non-verbal communication comprises the largest percentage of our communication. This refers to how we dress, how we sit, how we stand, shake hands, pay attention, etc. This is commonly referred to as "Body Language."

Our non-verbal communication is telling the prospect what we think of them, their company, our company, ourselves, our product, etc.

**Caution**

Our non-verbal communication plays a key role in our effectiveness at asking questions. The role it plays is in setting up a **Trusting Environment** for the prospect to feel safe in truthfully answering our questions.

Keep in mind when preparing to ask questions there are three levels of questions.

**First Level-**    Questions that are easy to answer, usually factual questions, usually short responses. Ususally safe because the prospect doesn't have to reveal any emotions or feelings. First level questions are important because they help the prospect feel comfortable.

DAVID L. SIMS

**Examples-** How long has your company been in business?

How many employees do you have?

What kinds of products or service do you provide?

How long have you been with the company?

List three additional First level questions.

1. _____

_____

2. _____

_____

3. _____

_____

**Second Level-** Second level questions go a little more in depth. They are most often essay questions that require a more lengthy response. However, they are still safe because the prospect doesn't have to reveal their **feelings** or **emotions**.

**Examples-** Tell me, what do like most about working with your company?

How did you come to be in the position you've achieved?

Describe a typical day at work.

List three Second level questions.

1. _____

_____

2. _____

_____

3. _____

_____

**Third Level-**     Third level questions are necessary to help in making the sale, especially high dollar sales. The third level questions are essay questions designed to generate **emotions** or **feelings**. Remember people buy emotionally.

**Examples-**     If I could solve your three greatest challenges, what would they be?

If we were meeting here three years from today and you were to look back over those three years to today, what has to have happened during that period, both personally and professionally, for you to feel our working together was successful?

Just suppose I could come in here and wave a magic wand and solve your greatest problem, what would it be?

List three Third level questions.

1. _____

_____

2. _____

_____

3. _____

_____

# CHAPTER 11
# YOU MUST HEAR WHAT'S IMPORTANT TO YOUR PROSPECT BEFORE YOU CAN OFFER A SOLUTION THEY WILL BUY.

**One of the greatest challenges most salespeople face is they feel they must talk the majority of the time. In reality, the formula should be just the reverse.**

Most people struggle with listening skills for several reasons. We have "not been taught to listen effectively." In school we listened for information to feed back, but we never had to listen for meaningful, emotional information.

The average American spends 2-4 hours a day behind a computer screen or a TV. Most TV is programmed so that we don't have to maintain a train of thought more than 6-8 minutes. Then there's a commercial break.

When people have not learned to ask **effective questions** they may talk to keep the conversation flowing. Then again, some people are so self-centered they feel the need to continually talk, thereby talking themselves out of the sale.

A good rule of thumb is for the sales person to talk 20-30% of the time. The prospect should talk 70-80% of the time. That means **you listen**.

# Requirements for Effective Listening Skills

1. Must truly care about people.

2. Must be able to ask effective, open-ended questions.

3. Focus your energy on the other person, not on yourself or distractions around you.

4. Be aware of your body language to make sure communication is not sabotaged. Be aware of the other person's body language to understand your emotions.

5. Ask for clarification if you are unsure of the emotion the person feels about the topic.

## Ten Tips For Listening Success

1. **Take notes** - Take notes about what you think their emotional buying signals are. Remember, pale ink is better than the best memory. Especially if you have several sales interviews each week.

2. **Listen now-report later** - One way to get people to open up is to ask effective questions and then listen. The greatest form of flattery for anyone is to have someone listening and seem genuinely interested in what they have to say.

3. **Learn to want to listen** - Sometimes you have to force yourself to listen. Remember the rewards. The more you talk "the fewer sales you'll make." The more the prospect talks "the more sales you'll make."

4. **Be present** - Focus on your prospect. You don't have to stare a hole in them but on the other hand, you don't want to be watch other people or looking around the room constantly.

5. **Anticipate excellence** - As you become more skilled at asking questions and listening you'll begin seeing excellent results. Your sales will go up and so will your self-confidence.

6. **Become a "Whole-body" listeners** - Be careful and aware of your body language. Ensure you don't have folded arms or showing other body language that indicates you're disinterested in what your prospect is saying.

7. **Build rapport by pacing the speaker** - If your prospect speaks fairly slowly, don't speak rapidly. Conversely if your prospect speaks fast, don't talk at a slow rate. It makes them feel uncomfortable.

8. **Control your emotional hot buttons** - If your prospect makes a statement you don't agree with you have to make a decision. "Do I want to make the sale, or do I want to get into an argument?"

9. **Control distractions** - It's very important to control interruptions if possible. If you're meeting in an office try to ensure you get not interruptions. I.e. phone calls or visitors. If you're meeting in a restaurant, try to get in a booth or at a table out of the mainstream traffic. You might even arrange with the wait staff to only come to your table when you request them.

10. **Feed back with questions** - Make sure you uncover the prospects "pain and prime buying motives." Don't hesitate to ask questions if you're unclear about what your prospect wants to accomplish, what they are willing to invest as far as time, effort, and money. But most important of all, "What will they benefit (their return on investment), from working with you.

# CHAPTER 12
# WHAT IS A PRIME BUYING MOTIVE?
# HOW DO YOU UNCOVER IT?
(You don't create pain, you uncover it.)

Prospects will become involved with your company for one of three reasons.

1. **Immediate need**. They have such a great need they are in pain. This is the easiest to sell.

2. **Fear** – The prospect has fear of a future event that could cause problems.

3. **Desire** – They want to gain something. Desire higher income, growth, a promotion, etc.

This step can be identified as the "pain/gain" step. It also can be referred to as finding the Prime Buying Motive. (In other words this is the number one reason your prospect would buy from you.)

The sales process is divided into two sections. The first section is the prospect presenting to you. They're presenting why you should do business with them. The second section of the process is you presenting to the prospect. You're presenting why they should do business with you. The division line is after the discovery step (prime buying motive, budget step, and decision step). In other words the first section ends after the Discovery step. Then the second half begins.

Most salespeople begin the process by presenting their product or service and hope the prospect is so overwhelmed with the "dynamic" presentation that they buy on the spot.

Or how about the "puppy dog" close? That's the pet storeowner letting you take the puppy home overnight. You or your child holds the puppy in your arms. The puppy wags its tail, licks your face and the next day you don't even ask how much. You just say, "We'll take it."

However, when you're in a sales situation and you present your product to a business owner before you have a clear picture of the discovery step (budget, need, and decision-making ability) your chances of making the sale are probably less than 20%.

Sales is all about <u>positioning</u> yourself in the process. How do you <u>position</u> yourself? The most effective way is by using effective questions.

## What are some factors that determine how well you are positioned?

1. One major factor is a referral. If you are introduced and recommended by someone having a lot of influence with the prospect you are well positioned.

2. If you are meeting the prospect via a cold call then you are positioned much differently in the eyes of the prospect. Not a very strong position.

3. Your ability to grab their attention with strong, effective introduction for you and your company.

4. Your skill at asking probing questions.

# Use Questions To Begin The Probing Process.

The beginning step is to do your homework and P.D.R. (practice, drill, and rehearse). (For you to learn and internalize these skills will take you from 750 to 1000 hours of practice in front of a prospect).

Your prospect probably has 4 to 6 challenges that they are continually faced with on a daily basis. Your product or service can probably address these issues and solve some problems for your prospect.

**Step 1:** Identify and internalize those 4 to 6 challenges.

You approach the prospect as follows:

**Step 2:** "Mr./Mrs. prospect, working with business owners/managers like yourself, I've found that you are continually challenged in four areas of your business."

 1. Employee turnover.

 2. Being able to find enough qualified workers.

 3. Employee morale.

 4. Employee productivity.

If I could help you fix your greatest challenge, which would benefit you the most? (The prospect could choose any one of the four but your response is always the same).

**Prospect:** Employee morale. If I had happier employees they would stay with the company longer, would be more productive, and would be happier.

**Your response:** That's a great choice, but tell me, why did you choose that one over number 1, 2, or 4?

**Prospect:** I think if we had higher morale that would solve many of our problems.

**Your Response:** Tell me, what do you see in your workforce that leads you to feel your employees morale is low?

Your prospect will begin telling you the challenges they have and then it's up to you to use your product or service to fix it for them.

This is one of the strategies used to help identify needs for the prospect.

You've now identified an area that is of concern to the prospect. (Remember you must have at least three (3) motives or pains to sell the prospect).

The next step is to utilize the selling funnel. Imagine a funnel. The wide mouth is at the top and the narrow opening is at the bottom. Your goal in the sales process is to begin by gathering general information about the prospect, their company, employees, or any other area. You then want to isolate a specific, emotional pain/gain that you can fix. This is represented by the narrow neck of the funnel. You're narrowing down and getting specific as to their buying needs.

# CHAPTER 13
# HELP YOUR PROSPECT SLIDE THROUGH
# THE SALES FUNNEL

There are five (5) steps in the process. We previously identified in the positioning section a way to find the first step. This five (5) step process is called the sales funnel.

## Sales Funnel

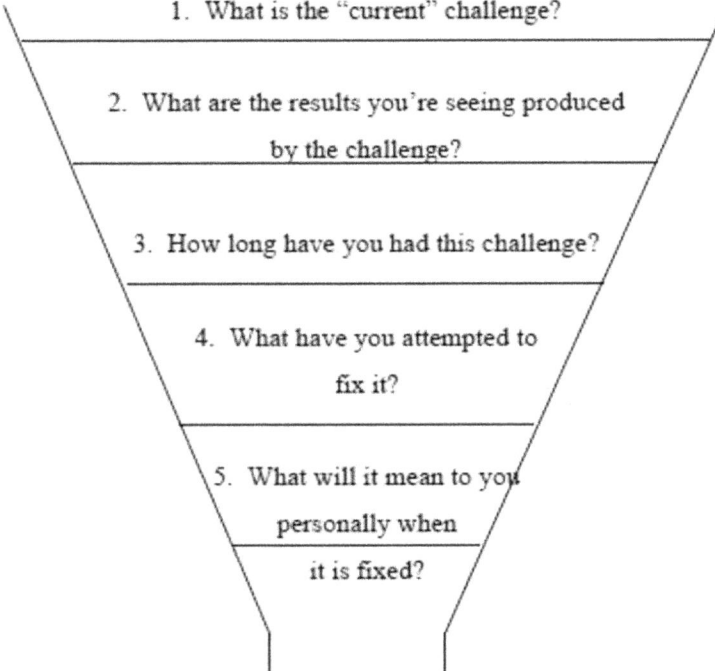

1. What is the "current" challenge?

2. What are the results you're seeing produced by the challenge?

3. How long have you had this challenge?

4. What have you attempted to fix it?

5. What will it mean to you personally when it is fixed?

**Step One.** Find the **current situation**. The most effective way to find the current situation is to ask "open-ended" essay questions. Effective questions can begin with, "who, what, when, where, and why."

Examples:

"Who is going to give you the greatest return on investment by being involved with additional training?"

"What is the biggest challenge you face daily running your department?"

"When it comes to investing resources where would you get the greatest R.O.I.?"

"Where is the greatest area of need?"

"Why are these important to you?"

# Step Two. Next, you must identify the **results** the situation is providing for the company. (The results you are looking for are challenges you have a solution for). The key to identifying the results being produced is to ask effective questions and get a picture of the challenges your prospect is facing. The results you'll be looking for are struggles or challenges for the person responsible. For example, the

person is a business owner and they say their sales have dropped off this quarter. That is step one or the current situation. Step two, or the results step, would sound like this:

**Salesperson:** "Mrs. Prospect, what effect does the low sales have on your organization?"

**Prospect:** There are many challenges. We may need to lay off people on the manufacturing side. This doesn't look good on my leadership skills. The sales people aren't going to be happy because their income is down.

**Step Three.** **How** **long** has this result been in existence? If the prospect tells you that they've been getting these results for years, then maybe it's not that important for him/her to fix it. Maybe they've made a decision that it's easier to live with it instead of going through the inconvenience of trying to fix the problem. You must find out if that's the case or not. Maybe they've had this problem and they didn't know there was a solution until you came along. You need to find out before going to the next step.

**Step Four.** What have you **attempted** to do to **correct** the situation? The important concept here is to see if the company has invested resources to solve the problem. If not, why not? If so, what kind of resources did they invest and what results did they produce?

**Step Five.** What will it mean to you **personally** when this is fixed? I remember asking a CEO for a medium sized company this question. His response was, "I don't care if this gets fixed or not because I'm retiring in 6 months." Needless to say, I didn't make the sale.

(This is the response that will tell you if you can sell to this prospect. If the prospect says it won't mean anything to them your chances of making a sale are limited. If they tell you many "emotional" reasons they want it fixed, then your chances are good).

Remember to become effective at selling to your prospect you need at least 2 or 3 good emotional reasons from the prospect to correct the problem.

# Questions to get started down the funnel.

Questions For Step 1

"If I could come into your organization and wave a magic wand and fix anything in your _____department for you, what would it be?" (Make sure the topic you insert in the blank is a service you offer.)

"Just suppose I could make your three biggest headaches disappear, what would they be?"

"If I could help you with three of your greatest challenges in your _____ department, what would they be?" (Again, ensure the question is designed to uncover a problem you can solve. If you offer accounting services then you would phrase your question as follows:

"Mr. prospect, if I could help you eliminate your three biggest challenges in your accounting department, what would they be?")

"You're happy with your current provider, and I don't blame you, they're an excellent company. But if they could do one thing just a little better, what would it be?"

"If we could help you in one area that would make a significant difference in your daily results, what would it be?"

Questions For Step 2

"What results are you seeing produced that leads you to feel you need to fine tune your:

"Organizational skills?"

"Copier service?"

"Computer service?"

"Delivery service?"

"Training service?"

Etc.

"When you say you feel your employee morale is low, what do you see happening to tell your that?"

"What do you see happening that tells you that you need help with your organizational skills?"

"When you say your employees production has slipped could you tell me what you see happening that leads you to that conclusion?"

"What leads you to feel that your computer network is costing you money?"

Questions For Step 3

"How long has this been happening?"

"What kind of time frame has passed since you first noticed this?"

"Could you tell me how long this has existed?"

"Could you tell me when you first noticed this occurring?

## Questions For Step 4

"What are some of the things you've done to attempt to correct this?"

"Could you tell me what you've done to address this issue?"

"What are some of the remedies you've used to address this situation?"

"What resources have you put toward this challenge?"

"In the past what were some of the different steps you've implemented to address this?"

## Questions For Step 5

"When this is fixed how will that affect you personally?"

"Just suppose I could provide a solution and it worked, how would that affect your day to day routine?"

"What will it mean to you when this is fixed?"

"How will this change your schedule when it is corrected?"

"If we were meeting 12 months from today, what would have to happen, both personally and professionally, for you to feel our time working together has been an excellent investment?"

# CHAPTER 14
# THE BUDGET STEP.

## DO THEY HAVE MONEY BUDGETED FOR YOUR PRODUCT OR SERVICE?

These two areas are the other components to the discovery step. This information plus the pain/gain is critical in the selling process.

How many times have you made a sales presentation and they seemed very interested until they realized they would have to invest money to purchase from you? That was the time you found out they hadn't budgeted any money.

It is paramount that you find out, before you present your product, if they have a budget. It is necessary to get it on the table to find out if there is money. The other important aspect is to get them thinking about the money process. What will happen if they don't have a budget set aside? You must find out two things.

First, are they willing to make a purchase?

Second, if they are willing to purchase and don't have a budget, where will they get the money?

There are three components of the discovery step.

- Pain/gain (need, etc.)
- Budget
- Decision-making process

It is easier to find the decision-making process and budget process after you've done a thorough needs-analysis.

# Questions to help uncover their budget.

**Salesperson:** "__, we've discussed several areas that could be opportunities for your growth. Let's say we went through the process and found a solution. How much do you have set aside in your budget for this?"

At this point there could be four possible responses.

1. They don't have a budget.

2. They have a budget but it's much less than you will be asking.

3. They have a budget and it's more than you're asking.

4. They have a budget but they are reluctant to share it with you.

We'll take each of these and propose ideas for you.

**Prospect:** "We don't have a budget."

**Salesperson:** "Joe, that's not unusual. But if we were to go through the process and find a workable solution that would exceed your goals 10, 20, 30%, you could find the money, couldn't you?"

**Prospect:** "Yes, I guess we could."

**Salesperson:** "Great, where would you get it?"

What if the "prospect" says "no, it's not in the budget and we can't do anything if it's not in the budget."

**Salesperson:** "Is money the real issue?"

**Prospect:** "Yes, money is the real issue."

**Salesperson:** "I'm confused, why would it be an issue? Is money the real issue or is it a belief issue?"

**Prospect:** "I don't understand."

**Salesperson:** "If you believed in your heart by us working together you could really exceed you goals, you couldn't find the money?"

**Prospect:** "If I really believed it, I could find the money."

**Salesperson:** "O.k. Where would you get it?"

**Prospect:** Responds.

# Different Scenario:

**Prospect:** "I would need to see how you're going to provide a solution."

**Salesperson:** "I'm assuming there's going to be a lot of things you've got to be comfortable with before you believe sufficiently to pay the kind of money we're asking."

**Prospect:** "Yeah."

**Salesperson:** "What are the major things?"

**Prospect:** Responds with 3-4 items.

**Salesperson:** "O.k. We'll build a plan, we'll go through the process. By the way, what form do you want that evidence?"

You also use this scenario if the prospect doesn't have nearly enough in their budget as your proposed solution will be.

# A "Yes" Will Make You  Rich
# A "No" Will Make You Rich
# "I Wanna Think It Over" Will Drive You Nuts And Out Of Business.

Usually if you're proposing a solution involving a large investment there will be more than one person involved in the decision-making process.  The larger the investment, the more that will be involved in the decision-making process. .  In many organizations the person you're proposing to could have a limit to the dollar amount they can authorize.

Sometimes you will be interviewing someone who is gathering information to take back to another individual or committee.  You must smoke all of this out before you begin your presentation of your proposed solutions.  How do you do this?  The best way is to be nurturing and softly ask questions.

**Salesperson:** "June, when it comes to making a decision about _____ _____, how is that handled in your organization?"

**Prospect:** "I make all decisions."

**Salesperson:** "You don't need any help?"

**Prospect:** "Nope, I make all the decisions."

**Salesperson:** "So if we found a solution and you felt it was worth all the time, effort, and money you would need to invest, you could make a decision <u>today</u>?"

**Prospect:** "Yes, I could."

**Salesperson:**  What do you need to see from me to make a yes decision?

At this point you can proceed.  You have to trust that the prospect is being up front with you.

What do you do if the prospect says, "Well, I can make a decision if the proposal solution doesn't exceed x-$."

**Salesperson:** "June, if the proposal will exceed x-$ who would help you with making the decision?"

**Prospect:** "I would take the information to Jill."

**Salesperson:** (softly) "May I make a suggestion?" Why don't we schedule a meeting between you, Jill, and myself. We'll go through the process and I can answer any questions either of you may have."

**Prospect:** "I'm supposed to gather the information and take it back to Jill."

**Salesperson:** "I can appreciate that. But here's what I've found. I've been involved in this industry for years. Whenever we get in a situation like this, this always happens. We'll go through the process and you'll take the information back to Jill. Jill will ask you a question about some issue we didn't cover. You won't know the answer and you'll feel not-o.k. about yourself. And I wouldn't want to put you in that position."

"What does your schedule and Jill's schedule look like for the next two weeks?"

What if the prospect is taking information back to a committee? This is a different game. You need to identify the decision-makers and influences on the committee. If you were recommend by someone on the committee you need to solicit that person to go to bat for you. Your result you want is an audience with the committee to present your proposal. It's necessary to present in person in order to be able to read the non-verbal cues given by the individuals.

# CHAPTER 15
# THE MOST EFFECTIVE WAY TO PRESENT HOW YOUR PRODUCT OR SERVICE WILL BE THE SOLUTION TO YOUR PROSPECT'S NEEDS.

Before you can begin the demonstration process it's imperative that you complete the discovery step.  If you start presenting your product or service before you complete the discovery step you'll probably close less than 10% of your sales.  This is equivalent to spilling your popcorn in the lobby.  If you do spill your popcorn in the lobby, you won't have any for the movie.

The demonstration begins with you.  You must be polite, self-confident, sympathetic, and well groomed.  Do you remember the old saying, "You never get a second chance to make a first impression?"  That is very true here.  Unfortunately many people feel their technical expertise will overcome their inattention to detail of their personal grooming.  In some instances this may be true but the vast majority of the time it's not.

(Put together a small booklet with the five following steps in it.  I had each person in the meeting one sheet at a time and go over the presentation packet that way.  If you hand them the entire booklet at one time the first thing they'll do is begin thumbing through it.  What are they looking for?  They're looking for how much this is going to cost and then that's all they can think about while you're presenting how you're going to solve their problem.)

**Step One:  About Your Company.**

This is a review about your company.  Usually your prospect has forgotten why he was talking with you unless you've done a great job of marketing.  You don't want to take any chances.  In this step you provide information about your company:

*Clients you've worked with. (Especially if they are high profile.)

*If you've been written up in any publications show the articles.

*Include a book of testimonials from excited clients.

*Anything that will build credibility for you and your company. (Note: Don't bore them to tears with a long drawn out show. Move through it quickly especially if you're presenting to a driver.)

**Step Two: Review The Prime Buying Motives With The Prospect.**

Review the 3-4 emotional needs you've uncovered with the prospect. Get an agreement the problems you've uncovered are the major ones and what they want fixed. Your statement might go like this. "Mr. prospect these are the three areas I heard you wanted fixed. Did I hear you correctly?" When they agree you can proceed. If they say "No" they are not the three. He/she has some other issues. You then need to begin over with the process.

**Step Three: List The Services You Will Provide To Solve Their Problems.**

In this step you demonstrate step-by-step how your product or service will provide the solution for their challenges. If you have a product to demonstrate get the client as involved as possible. If you use charts, overheads, etc. make sure they appear professional, are well done, simple, easy to understand, and proves your point. If you're talking numbers, give them a calculator and have them do the math. This implants the number in their minds.

If you are presenting close to your prospect with an item such as a manual or booklet, use a nice pen or pointer instead of your hand or fingers. If you use your hands quite a lot make sure they are well groomed.

As you move through the presentation point out the ways your product will solve their problem. Also get confirmation they agree your solution will work.

Ask questions along the way such as:

- Of the information you've seen so far which do you feel is the most beneficial? Why?

- Of the material you've seen to this point what's the best idea you've gotten?

- Of the material you've seen to this point what do you think will work best for you? Why?

As you wrap up the demonstration. You then move into the close. A good technique to transition from the demonstration to the close is to simply ask:

- "Mr. Prospect, I sense you feel this is a good solution to your challenge, what do you want me to do next?"

- "Mr. Prospect, what's the next step?"

**Selling Tips:**

- Don't show them something they didn't mention.

- Never answer a question they didn't ask.

**Step Four: The Results Step. List the results they can expect to enjoy.**

Review the results your prospect can expect to achieve after they make a decision to go with you. You want to create an Irresistible Offer the prospect will have a hard time turning down.

**Step Five: The Investment Step. (Break down the investment for**

them. One of the effective tactics I use is to offer more than one solutions. If you only have one offer then their decision can only be a "yes" or a "no." If you offer them more than one option you change their thinking. Don't offer more than three or they'll get confused and a confused mind "always says NO.")

This is the step you provide them with the amount of investment it will cost to implement your proposed solution. Some people will insist that you want to talk about money first and solve that problem. I choose to wait until last to provide the investment so I can focus on building value and delivery.

# CHAPTER 16
# CLOSING THE SALE.
# THE MOST EFFECTIVE WAY TO GET
# YOUR PROSPECT TO CLOSE YOU.

Closing is the step most salespeople fear. This is usually the step where people talk about money. Many salespeople avoid this step because by not asking the prospect to buy the prospect can't say "NO." The main factor that will make the closing step easier is to do an excellent job in the "Discovery Step." (Finding the Prime Buying Motive, The Budget, and The Decision-Making Process.)

The "close" is the "logical" conclusion to the sales process. If the prior steps have been adhered to the "close" is wrapping up of the details.

The close is the logical conclusion to an effective sales presentation. There are many books available on the subject of closing. There are courses available to learn 100 to 150 closes. You need very few.

Another challenge salespeople have is to know the right time to close. Timing is a critical issue. The best way to know the precise time to close is to have the prospect close the salesperson.

Let's role-play to see how this would work. Before we role-play we must first describe the scenario. You've done an excellent job in all the steps prior to the discovery step. In the discovery step you've found the company does have a budget set aside for your product. You're talking to the decision-maker.

## You've Found A Prime Buying Motive

1. You've found they're losing $50,000.00 a month because of the poor service they're currently receiving.

2. The decision-maker's job is on the line unless he produces different results in the next 12 months.

3. The decision-maker is stressed and the time he's spending with his family is limited.

Also, prior to the closing step you've demonstrated how your product or service will solve their problem. You've reviewed all the pains the decision-maker is challenged with. You know who the decision makers are.

## The Closing Step

# (close 1)

**Salesperson:** Joe, we've reviewed the needs you have and you've agreed that our service will solve your problem. Is that correct?

**Joe:** Yes, it is.

**Salesperson:** Joe, are there any areas we missed or didn't talk about that you'd like to discuss?

**Joe:** No, I think we've covered them all.

**Salesperson:** Great Joe. What do you want me to do next?

# (close 2)

**Salesperson:** Joe, what's the next step?

**Joe:** What do I need to do to subscribe to your service?

**Salesperson:** Joe, do you want to get started today?

**Joe:** Yes, I want to get started. The sooner I begin, the quicker I'll begin seeing results.

(If you ask, "when do you want to get started," and they respond, "yesterday," you know you've done an excellent job in the discovery step.)

# CLOSES

These are the only closes you need if you do a great job in the discovery step.

- What's the next step?
- What do you want me to do?
- If I could find a solution to your challenge when would be the latest you would want to begin?

## Thermometer close (This is a great technique to use for gauging any part of the process. For example you could ask, "Mr. prospect just how interested are you in our offer? On a scale of one to ten with one being you have no interest what so ever, and ten being you want to buy now, where are you?)

**Salesperson:** Jill, on a scale of 1 to 10 with 1 being you want me to pack my bags this moment and get out. And 10 being you're going to place an order and write me a check, where do you feel you'd fall on that scale?

(If the prospect responds with a number of 6 or below you haven't done a good job in the discovery step. You have to back up, regroup and begin again in the process. However, if they respond 7 to 10 you're chance of making a sale is pretty good.)

**Jill:** I'd say I'm a 7.

**Salesperson:** Jill, what would you need to see from me to move you to a 10?

**Jill:** I need to see how the terms will fit our plan. How your equipment stacks up against company ABC. And verify the responsiveness of your service department.

**Salesperson:** I'll be happy to get all that information together for you. Once I've presented and you agree we can do what we say we can do, at that time would you be willing to go ahead with the project?

**Jill:** Yes, I will.

**Salesperson:** Great, let's set a time to get back together so I can present to you.

# CHAPTER 17
# HOW TO OVERCOME STALLS AND OBJECTIONS

An "objection" usually is a prospect's way to request more information. A "stall" is a put off because the prospect struggles with making decisions. Prospects disguise stalls and objections with many different techniques.

- I want to think about it.

- Your price is too high.

- The timing's not right.

- This may not fit into our marketing plan.

- We don't have money in the budget.

The list could be endless.

The major concept to remember is that an objection is a "request for more information." So instead of a prospect saying something like, "based on the information available to me I don't have sufficient information to make an accurate decision." They'll say, "Your price is to high for our budget."

## Techniques For Overcoming Stalls And Objections

The critical factor is to **isolate** the stall or objection. You want to make sure you're dealing with the real issue and not a smoke screen. If you're dealing with a smoke screen and answer that objection then the prospect will generate another one.

## Isolate the Objection or Stall

**Salesperson:** John, you say you like our product and feel we have a solution that will help your company grow. What do you want me to do next?

133

**John:** Tell me how much it is going to cost me.

**Salesperson:** One million dollars.

**John:** That's too much money.

**Salesperson:** That's more than you're willing to invest?

**John:** That's correct.

**Salesperson:** John, do you mind if I ask you a question?

**John:** No, go ahead.

**Salesperson:** John, if we could solve the money issue, would you make a decision to go ahead today?

**John:** Yes, I would.

**Salesperson:** What do we need to do to solve this issue?

**John:** Do you have some kind of terms we can work out because we just don't have that in our budget?

## Feel, Felt, Found Technique

**Prospect:** You're asking way too much money for your service.

**Salesperson:** How much too much?

**Prospect:** About 10%.

**Salesperson:** John, I can understand how you **feel**. Many of our clients have **felt** the same way before we started working with them. Here's what they **found**. The quality of the products, the responsiveness and quality of service, and the extra value we provide for our customers is well worth the extra 10%. I would be happy to connect you with some of our customers to verify the extra value.

**John:** That won't be necessary.

**Salesperson:** We can get you involved with our process this week or next, which is the best for you?

# Belief Objection

This technique could be one of the most powerful available. The belief (or lack of belief) falls into three areas:

1. They don't believe you can do what you say you can.

2. They don't believe your product or service will do what you say.

3. They lack belief in themselves. They don't believe they can make your system work. Whatever objection your prospect gives you, you can counter with this technique.

**Prospect:** You're asking too much money.

**Salesperson:** Jana, is money the real issue here?

**Jana:** Most certainly, way too much money.

**Salesperson:** Jana, is money the real issue of is it a belief issue?

**Jana:** What do you mean?

**Salesperson:** Jana, we talked about your challenges in the discovery steps. You have some that are significant. If you truly believed and had the conviction that our system would solve your problems you'd find the money, wouldn't you?

**Jana:** I guess I could.

**Salesperson:** O.k. What do you need from me?

Some of the most common objectives are time, effort, money, and energy. This technique is extremely effective in handling these challenges.

## Time Kills Deals

**"In order for someone to buy from you they have to feel better about themselves after you leave then when you were with them."** 80% to 90% live their lives in a "Negative environment." When you are around them they are in a "Positive environment" because of your upbeat attitude and personality.

Imagine a scale of "1 to 10" with the number "10" representing a sale. When you are with your prospect they begin moving up the "Positive" scale because they are in a positive state. When you leave there's nothing to maintain the positive atmosphere so they lose their enthusiasm and desire to make a change.

The more time that passes between you're meeting with them and them making a decision to buy, the more likely they will say "No." "Time Kills Deals." Imagine a scale of "1 to 10." You need to move them up to at least a "7" to get them in the mood to buy. Each time you leave it's critical you have a "next step" of something to do to ensure you get back together.

It might be another meeting. It might be that you're going to provide them with some information. Maybe they're going to provide you with some numbers or documentation, etc. Each time you have a "Next step" in the process you'll move up the "positive scale." This will keep you in the sales process as long as you can keep them going up the scale.

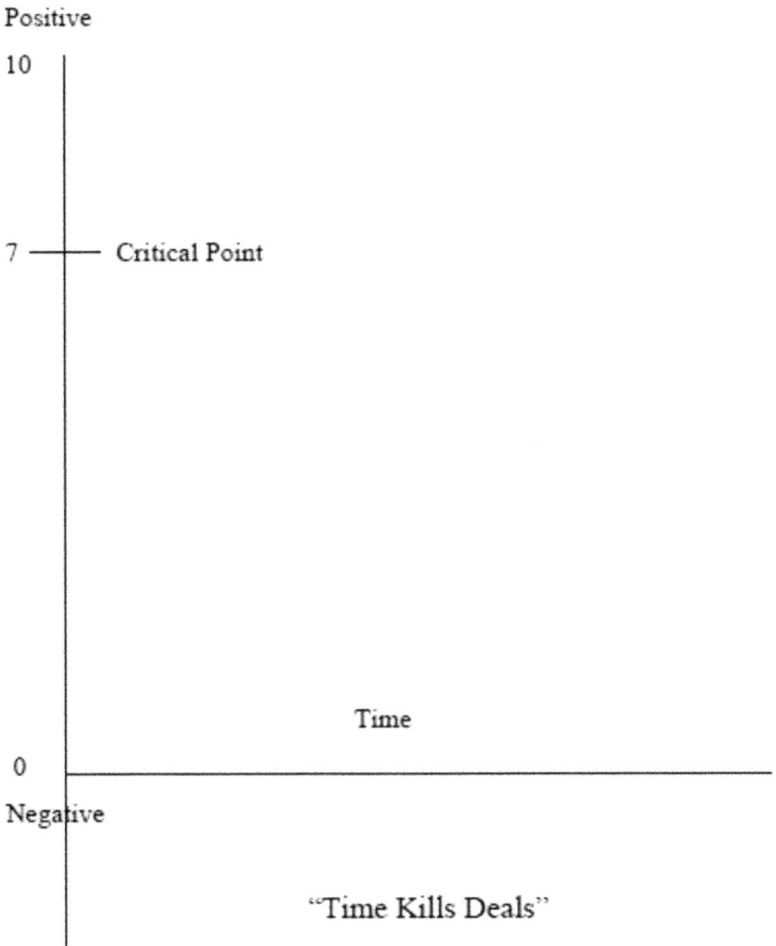

"Time Kills Deals"

# SUMMARY

Selling is one of the best professions you can develop. I've been a medical worker, photographer, a sawyer in a lumberyard, a stock boy in a feed store and many other odd jobs. I never really enjoyed a good income until I began working in sales.

Selling is a skill like any other. It can be learned. Are there some people better in sales than others? Absolutely. Are there better basketball players, baseball players, football players, etc. than others? Sure. But you can still compete and earn an excellent income if you have the desire and you're willing to put the effort in to practice, drill, and rehearse to learn the sales process.

If you want to write your own ticket and create your own destiny, then selling is the profession you should choose. After all, if I can be successful at selling anyone can do it.

Remember "Eagles Soar-Turkeys Get Eaten

Soar With The Eagles

David L. Sims

www.ingramcontent.com/pod-product-compliance
Lightning Source LLC
Chambersburg PA
CBHW051536170526
45165CB00002B/750